HOW●
REAL
IS
REAL?

HOW REAL IS REAL?

Confusion
Disinformation
Communication

PAUL WATZLAWICK

Vintage Books
A Division of Random House
New York

Vintage Books Edition, February 1977

Library of Congress Cataloging in Publication Data

Watzlawick, Paul.
How real is real?

Includes bibliographical references and index.
1. Communication.   2. Reality.   I. Title.
[P91.W3 1977]   301.14   76-40476
ISBN 0-394-72256-6

Grateful acknowledgments are made to the following authors:

Professor John C. Wright, University of Kansas, Lawrence, for his additional information on noncontingent reward experiments;

Dr. Roger S. Fouts, University of Oklahoma, Norman, for his permission to refer to a forthcoming publication;

the Honorable Ewen E. S. Montagu, CBE, QC, DL, London, for his kind help in checking on my presentation of Operation Mincemeat;

Dr. Bernard M. Oliver, Vice President, Research and Development, Hewlett-Packard Company, Palo Alto, for his extensive advice on problems of extraterrestrial communication and his permission to reproduce the coding and decoding of a sample message.

The illustrations are by courtesy of Ann A. Wood.

Contents

Foreword

This book is about the way in which communication creates what we call reality. At first glance this may seem a most peculiar statement, for surely reality is what is, and communication is merely a way of expressing or explaining it.

Not at all. As the book will show, our everyday, traditional ideas of reality are delusions which we spend substantial parts of our daily lives shoring up, even at the considerable risk of trying to force facts to fit our definition of reality instead of vice versa. And the most dangerous delusion of all is that there is only one reality. What there are, in fact, are many different versions of reality, some of which are contradictory, but all of which are the results of communication and not reflections of eternal, objective truths.

The close connection between reality and communication is a relatively new idea. Although physicists and engineers long ago solved the problems of transmitting signals effectively, and although linguists have for centuries been engaged in exploring the origin and structure of language, and semanticists have been delving into the meanings of signs and symbols, the pragmatics of communication—that is, the ways in which people can drive each other crazy and the very different world views that can arise as a consequence of communication—have become an independent area of research only in the past decades.

It is my unabashed intention to entertain the reader by presenting in anecdotal form certain selected subjects from this new field of scientific investigation—subjects that are, I hope, unusual, intriguing and yet of very practical, direct importance in explaining how different views of reality arise and what human conflicts are about.

Some of the examples used, which are taken from fiction, jokes, games and puzzles, may seem frivolous, but they should not mask the underlying seriousness of the enterprise. There are two methods of scientific explanation. One is to expound a theory and then show how observable facts bear it out.* The other is to present examples from many different contexts to make obvious, in a very practical way, the structure that they have in common and the conclusions that follow from them. In the first approach, the examples are used as proof. In the second, their function is metaphorical and illustrative—they are meant to demonstrate something, to translate it into a more familiar language, but not necessarily to prove anything.

I have chosen the second approach, and through it I hope

---

* An excellent example of this form of presentation of the same subject matter is *The Social Construction of Reality*, by Peter L. Berger and Thomas Luckman (Doubleday, 1966).

to enable the reader to enter the complex field of reality formation by the back door so to speak. No prior knowledge of the subject matter is necessary; no theories or formulas are given. But the bibliography in the back provides the necessary references and source materials for anyone who wants to probe more deeply into any of the areas suggested here. I like to think that the student of the social or behavioral sciences may perhaps find in these pages some ideas for a research project or a subject for his dissertation.

I hope that the book may serve another function as well. As I have already said, the belief that one's own view of reality is the only reality is the most dangerous of all delusions. It becomes still more dangerous if it is coupled with a missionary zeal to enlighten the rest of the world, whether the rest of the world wishes to be enlightened or not. To refuse to embrace wholeheartedly a particular definition of reality (e.g., an ideology), to dare to see the world differently, can become a "think-crime" in a truly Orwellian sense as we get steadily closer to 1984. I would like to think that this book might contribute, if only in a small way, to creating an awareness of those forms of psychological violence which might make it more difficult for the modern mind-rapists, brainwashers and self-appointed world saviors to exert their evil power.

My original training in modern languages and philosophy, my years of practical experience in criminal investigation and security work, and especially my twenty-four years as a clinical psychotherapist, fourteen of them spent as a research associate and investigator at the Mental Research Institute in Palo Alto, an institution devoted to the study of interpersonal communication and its disturbances in families and larger social contexts, have given me direct contact with most of the material presented here. Other parts of the book are based on my teaching and consulting activities as clinical assistant professor of psychiatry at Stanford University and guest lecturer at various universities and psychiatric research or training institutes in the United States, Canada, Latin America and Europe. Some of the subjects mentioned in the book I know only indirectly and theoretically, but needless to say, the responsibility for any errors rests exclusively with me.

The book is divided into three parts. Part I deals with *confusion;* that is, those breakdowns of communication and attendant distortions that arise involuntarily. Part II examines the somewhat exotic concept of *disinformation,* by which I mean such knots, impasses and delusions as may come about in the voluntary process of actively seeking or of deliberately withholding information. Part III is devoted to the fascinating problems involved in establishing *communication* in areas where none is as yet in existence—that is, of creating a reality that can usefully be shared by human and other beings, especially animals and extraterrestrials.

It is my pleasant duty to thank William B. O'Boyle for a generous gift to the Mental Research Institute, which made possible the rapid production of the final manuscript, and Claire Bloom for her untiring help in its technical preparation.

P.W.

PART I
Confusion

1

The Trials
of Translation

. . . let us go down and there confound their language, that they may not understand one another's speech.

Genesis 11:7

All living things depend on adequate information about their environment in order to survive; in fact, the great mathematician Norbert Wiener once suggested that the world "may be viewed as a myriad of To Whom It May Concern messages." The exchange of these messages is what we call communication. And when one of the messages is garbled, leaving the recipient in a state of uncertainty, the result is confusion, which produces emotions ranging all the way from mild bewilderment to acute anxiety, depending upon the circumstances. Naturally, when it comes to human relations and human interaction, it is especially important to maximize understanding and minimize confusion. To repeat here an often quoted remark by Hora: "To understand himself, man needs to be understood by another. To be

understood by another, he needs to understand the other"
[73].°

Confusion is not usually dealt with as a subject in its own
right, especially by students of communication. It is something bad, to be got rid of. But because it is, in a sense, a
mirror image of "good" communication, it can teach us
quite a bit about our successes as well as our failures in
reaching one another.

Translation from one language to another offers an
unusually fertile field for confusion. This extends far beyond
plain translation mistakes and simply bad translations. Much
more interesting is the confusion caused by the different
meanings of identical or similar words. *Burro,* for example,
means "butter" in Italian and "ass" in Spanish, and this is
responsible for a number of weird misunderstandings—at
least in the punch lines of Hispano-Italian jokes. Chiavari
(with the accent on the first *a*) is a beautiful resort on the
Italian Riviera; *chiavare* (accented on the second *a*) is
Italian vernacular for love-making. Needless to say, this
provides the *pointe* for a number of somewhat raunchy
jokes, all involving tourists who cannot pronounce Italian.
Somewhat more serious and less forgivable is the amazingly
frequent confusion of words like the French *actuel* (the
equivalent of the Spanish *actual,* Italian *attuale,* German
aktuell, etc.), which sounds the same as the English *actual*
(in its sense of "real" or "factual") but means "present," "at
this time" and even "up to date." The same is true of the
French *eventuellement* (Spanish and Italian *eventualmente*
and German *eventuell*), which has nothing to do with the
English *eventually* (in its meaning of "finally" or "in the
end") but means "possibly," "perhaps." Considerably more

° The numbers in square brackets throughout the text refer to the
sources listed in the comprehensive Bibliographical Notes at the end of
the book.

serious is the frequent mistake committed by translators with the number word *billion*, which in the United States and France means a thousand millions (10^9) but in England and most continental European countries it means a million millions (10^{12}). There the U.S. billion is called *miliardo*, *Milliarde*, etc. The reader will appreciate that confusion between butter and an ass is of minor consequence, but the difference between 10^9 and 10^{12} can mean disaster if hidden in, say, a textbook on nuclear physics.

This confusion about meanings, incidentally, is not limited to humans, as the book of Genesis implies. Bees, we know from the pioneering investigations of Nobel Prize-winning scientist Karl von Frisch, have complex and efficient dance "languages," which differ from one species to another. Since the species cannot interbreed, no language confusion can arise between them. There is, however, a startling exception, which von Frisch discovered several years ago, involving the Austrian and Italian bees [46]. They are members of the same species and can therefore interbreed, but while they speak the same language, they use different "dialects" in which certain messages have a different meaning. When a bee has found a source of food, she returns to the hive and there performs a peculiar dance which not only alerts the others to her discovery but also tells them the quality and location. Von Frisch found that there are three dances involved:

1. If a nectar source is quite near the hive, the bee performs a *round dance*, consisting in alternating circles to the right and left.

2. If the source is at an intermediate distance, the bee goes into a *sickle dance*, so called because it resembles a flattened figure 8 bent into a semicircle, which looks like a sickle. The opening of the sickle points in the direction of the food, and as always in bee dances, the speed of the dance indicates the quality of the nectar.

3. If the source is farther away, the bee attracts the attention of her hive-mates by a *wagging dance,* moving for a few centimeters in a straight line toward the target, and then returning to the starting point and repeating the movement. While moving in the direction of the source, the bee wags her abdomen.

The Italian bee uses the wagging dance for distances of more than forty meters, but for the Austrian bee this dance means a much longer distance. Thus an Austrian bee, acting on the information supplied by an Italian hive-mate, will search for the food too far away. Conversely, an Italian bee will not fly far enough when alerted to food by the wagging of an Austrian colleague.

Bee languages are innate, not learned. When von Frisch produced Austro-Italian hybrids, he found that sixteen of them had body markings very much like their Italian parent but "spoke Austrian" in that they used the sickle dance to indicate intermediate distances 65 out of 66 times. Fifteen hybrids that looked like their Austrian parent used the round dance 47 out of 49 times when they meant the same distance. In other words, they "spoke Italian."

What is most significant about this example is that we humans run into precisely the same kind of confusion when we use body language, which is "inherited" through tradition and which we are almost totally unaware of unless we see a member of a different culture use it differently, in a way that seems to us odd or wrong. Members of any given society share myriads of behavior patterns that were "programmed" into them as a result of growing up in that particular culture, subculture and family tradition, and some of these patterns may not have the same connotations to an outsider. The ethnologists tell us that there are literally hundreds of ways of, for instance, greeting another person or expressing joy or grief in different cultures. It is one of the basic laws of communication that all behavior in the presence of another person has message value, in the sense that it defines and modifies the relationship between these people. All behavior says something; for example, total silence or lack of reaction clearly implies, "I don't want to have anything to do with you." And since this is so, it is easy to see how much room there is for confusion and conflict.

In every culture, there is a very specific distance that two strangers will maintain between each other in a face-to-face encounter.° In Central and Western Europe and in North America, this is the proverbial arm's length, as the reader can easily verify by inviting any two people to walk up to each other and stop at the "right" distance. In Mediterranean countries and in Latin America, the distance is considerably shorter. Thus, in an encounter between a North American and a South American, both try to take up what they consider the right distance. The Latin moves up; the Northerner backs away to what he unconsciously feels is the proper distance; the Latin, feeling uncomfortably distant, moves closer, etc. Both feel that the other is somehow behaving wrongly and try to "correct" the situation, creating a typical human problem in which the corrective behavior of one partner inspires a reverse correction by the other [183]. And since in all probability there is nobody around who could translate their respective body languages for them, they are in a worse situation than the unsuccessfully searching bees, for they will blame each other for their discomfort.

A dramatic example of this can be found in Laing, Phillipson and Lee's book, *Interpersonal Perception* [81]:

> A husband and wife, after eight years of marriage, described one of their first fights. This occurred on the

° Standing side by side is a different matter; in most cultures it is all right to come very close and even to rub elbows, provided the arms are not bare.

second night of their honeymoon. They were both sitting at a bar in a hotel when the wife struck up a conversation with a couple sitting next to them. To her dismay her husband refused to join the conversation, remained aloof, gloomy and antagonistic both to her and the other couple. Perceiving his mood, she became angry at him for producing an awkward social situation and making her feel "out on a limb." Tempers rose, and they ended in a bitter fight in which each accused the other of being inconsiderate.

Now, eight years later, they discover that they had approached the situation "honeymoon" with two very different interpretations, naïvely assuming that, "of course," it had the same meaning in the other's "language" as well. For the wife, the honeymoon was the first opportunity to practice her newly acquired social role: "I have never had a conversation with another couple as a wife before. Previous to this I had always been a 'girl friend' or 'fiancée' or 'daughter' or 'sister.'"

The husband's interpretation of "honeymoon," however, was of a period of exclusive togetherness, a "golden opportunity," as he put it, "to ignore the rest of the world and simply explore each other." For him, his wife's conversation with the other couple meant that he was insufficient to fill her demands. And again, there was no interpreter who could have spotted their "translation mistake."

Even with the largely conscious uses of verbal language, a translator in the usual sense of the term (that is, a person who is trained to transpose meaning from one spoken language into another) needs to know much more than the languages involved. Translating is an art, and even a bad human translator is much better than the best translating machine in existence. But it is a frustrating art, for even the best translation entails a loss—perhaps not so much of objective information as of that intangible essence of any language, its beauty, imagery and metaphors for which there is no one-to-one translation.

The Italians have a famous saying, *Traduttore, traditore*, an expression that is in itself a pithy example of the difficulty it describes. As the famous linguist Roman Jacobson once remarked, if one were to translate this epigram into English as "The translator is a traitor," one would strip it of its paranomastic° value. In other words, it is a correct translation, but it is not what the original means.

An additional problem lies in the fact that language not only conveys information but also expresses a world view. The nineteenth-century linguist Wilhelm von Humboldt once remarked that different languages are not so many designations of the same thing; they are different views of it. This becomes particularly evident in international meetings where ideologies clash and the interpreter who speaks the languages but does not understand the ideologies finds himself hopelessly at sea. A democracy is not exactly the same thing as a people's democracy; *détente* means something very different in the Soviet vocabulary than it does in that of NATO; one and the same thing may be called "liberation" by some and "enslavement" by others.

Thus the translator, and even more the interpreter, who must make his decisions in split seconds without the help of dictionaries, may inadvertently trigger vast consequences, either from very minor mistakes or from a well-meant attempt to "clarify." Professor Robert Ekvall, an interpreter of Oriental languages, who for many years participated in the most sensitive diplomatic negotiations in the Far East, has described a classic example of this:

In the final session of the Geneva conference on Korea, in the summer of 1954, Paul Henri Spaak was the spokesman

° From *paranomasia:* to call a slight change of name, a play on words.

for the United Nations against the intransigence of North Korea, China (represented by Chou En-lai) and the USSR. Spaak felt that

> the comprehensiveness and truthfulness of the United Nations proposal made it superfluous to consider any other proposal and so he finished with the statement: *"Cette déclaration est contenue dans notre texte."* [This statement is contained in our text.] The simultaneous English version that came into my other ear said: "This statement is contained in the text of the armistice agreement." It later was discovered that the interpreter had heard the words *"dans notre texte"* as *"dans l'autre texte"* [in the other text] and thinking that *"l'autre"* was vague and needed explanation, had added his own clarification by inserting the words "of the armistice agreement."

From here on matters escalated. Chou began to accuse Spaak of having made a groundless assertion, pointing out that contrary to what Spaak had said, the proposal of the delegation of the People's Republic of China was *not* a part of the armistice agreement.

Paul Henri Spaak was watching Chou En-lai with an expression of mildly interested detachment mixed with obvious wonderment as to just what all the fuss was about. Also, perhaps, thinking that the shrill Chinese syllables were a strange answer to the nuanced beauty of what had been so well said in French, yet willing to learn what those unfamiliar syllables meant, he adjusted his earphones with good-natured intent. But when their meaning, passed from Chinese through English into French, finally reached his understanding, it was his turn to start angrily and with hand and voice begin asking for the floor.

The delegates who had listened to Spaak's original

statement in French were bewildered by Chou's reaction, while those who had only the "enriched" Chinese translation to go by (the Chinese and the North Koreans) obviously found Spaak's indignation inappropriate.

The next development was yet another translation mistake. Spaak managed to get the point across that he had never said the fateful words "of the armistice agreement," and as so often happens in the aftermath of a breakdown in communication, both he and his former adversary tried to outdo each other in their eagerness to explain and make matters clear once and for all. Chou then said:

> If the declaration put forward by the sixteen United Nations states and the last proposal put forward by the delegation of the People's Republic of China, *though having a few certain differences,* come from a common desire, instead of having a unilateral declaration by the sixteen, why cannot the nineteen states represented at this Geneva Conference express this common desire in a common agreement?

The crucial phrase in this statement was obviously the one in italics, but since the heat was now on the translators, Chou's interpreter slipped and omitted these key words, which qualified and limited the entire statement.

> What Spaak finally heard in French was a sweeping plea for agreement based on a common desire for settlement. It possibly sounded even like a belated Chinese acceptance of the point of view he had defended so eloquently. He may have felt that at last he had persuaded Chou to be reasonable. In the heated exchanges of misunderstanding he had passed beyond the point of cold, hard thinking and, eager to show that he too was reasonable, his impulses spoke.
> *"En ce que me concerne et pour éviter toute doute, je suis prêt à affirmer que j'accepte la proposition du délégué de la*

république chinoise." [As far as I am concerned, and in order to avoid any doubt, I am ready to state that I accept the proposition of the delegate of the Chinese Republic.]

The results were nothing short of sensational. Bedlam broke out. Spaak, the great and respected leader of the Western world, had "virtually" betrayed his side, had broken away—to quote Ekvall—

> from the agreement and unity so carefully arrived at before the final meeting and had gone over to the enemy. Prime Minister Casey of Australia, Vice President Garcia of the Philippines, and heads of other delegations were all asking for the floor. General Bedell Smith, chief of the United States delegation, was trying to do two things at the same time: get the floor, and by actual physical restraint hold the delegation of South Korea in place, for that delegation, suddenly convinced of treachery, had started to walk out. Sir Anthony Eden, caught up in the confusion of the developments, obviously didn't know whether Spaak had given ground or had wrung an unexpected concession from the Chinese. Nor could he be sure to whom of many claimants he should grant the floor, and thus he, too, seemed to give ground in uncertainty. [38]

What Ekvall only hints at is that since he knew all the languages used, he was probably the only person in the entire plenary session of this decisive international meeting who had noticed the origins of the confusion and all the stages of its subsequent escalation. But the function of the interpreter is relegated to that of a "faithful echo," as Ekvall modestly puts it, and no interpreter is permitted to take an active part in the proceedings. This is, of course, quite appropriate as far as the negotiations *as such* go. But as far as the flow of communication is concerned, the interpreter is in an even more important position than the chairman.

Like any go-between, the interpreter has a great deal of secret power.° Both sides need him, and neither side can (usually) control him. The temptation to be more than a faithful echo is at times great. There is an old story, going back to the days of the Austro-Hungarian Empire, about an army detachment advancing toward an Albanian village. The commandant has orders to carry out punitive action if certain Austrian demands are not fully met by the villagers. As it happens, none of the Austrians knows any Albanian, and none of the villagers speaks any of the many languages used interchangeably in the Austro-Hungarian army. Finally, an interpreter is found. He happens to be richly endowed with the expertise in dealing with human nature that distinguishes the inhabitants of those lands to the east and south of Vienna. There is hardly a sentence in the lengthy negotiation that he translates correctly. Instead he tells each side what it wants to hear or is prepared to accept, slipping in a minor threat here, a promise there, until both sides find the other so reasonable that the Austrian officer sees no point in insisting on his demands, while the villagers will not let him go until he has accepted what he is led to believe are voluntary retributions, but which they consider parting gifts.

At the time this story allegedly took place, the term psychotherapy had not yet been invented, but what the interpreter did is obviously of a therapeutic nature. This

° A good example is the Parsees, who, after having been driven from their Persian homeland by the advance of Islam, led an isolated minority existence among the Marathi- and Gujarati-speaking population of what is now the greater Bombay area, and of necessity learned both languages. With the arrival of the East India Company and subsequently the British colonial administration, they became mediators between the British and the local population, especially as suppliers, ship's chandlers, traders, etc., amassing enormous fortunes and gaining great influence without ever ceasing to be a small minority.

may seem to the reader a strange use of the term, since it is a far cry from exploring the unconscious mind and gaining insight. The story in fact depicts a web of lies, calculated manipulations and deliberate confusion. But let us ask ourselves the crucial question: Which situation was the more confused and therefore "sicker"—the one existing before or after the interpreter's intervention? At what price "honesty"?

We will have to return to this question and its questionable answers later, when discussing those strange contexts of communication where everything is true, and so is its contrary. For the time being, let me suggest only that a better understanding of communication not only gives us a new view of problems, it also forces us to question our old ways of dealing with them.

2

Paradoxes

To think that I am not going
to think of you any more
is still thinking of you.
Let me then try not to think
that I am not going to think of you.

Zen saying

Translation is by no means the primary source of confusion. Sometimes confusion is inherent in the structure of the message itself. Again, this is best introduced by examples:

1. According to a very ancient story, which has vexed philosophers and theologians alike, the devil once questioned God's omnipotence by asking Him to create a rock so enormously big that even God Himself could not lift it. What was God to do? If He cannot lift the rock, He is no longer omnipotent; if He can lift it, He is unable to make it big enough.

2. When asked what he thought that Mona Lisa smiled about, an eight-year-old is supposed to have said, "Well, one evening when Mr. Lisa came home from work, he asked her, 'What kind of a day did you have, dear?' And Mona Lisa smiled and said, 'Imagine, Leonardo da Vinci came and painted my portrait.'"

15

3. There is a popular bumper sticker that reads: "My convictions are not for public display."

4. "I'm glad I don't like cauliflower, because if I did, I'd eat it, and I hate the stuff." (Anonymous)

5. The philosopher Karl Popper claims, tongue in cheek, that he once sent the following letter to a colleague:

Dear M.G.,

Kindly return this card to me, but make sure to write "Yes," or to put some other mark of your choice, in the blank rectangle to the left of my signature if, and only if, you feel justified in predicting that, upon its return, I shall find this space still empty.

Yours sincerely,

K. R. Popper [134]

If by now the reader feels a strange paralysis creeping into his mind, he has already had a direct experience of this form of confusion. Let us look at still another example, this one from *Mary Poppins*, by Pamela L. Travers. Mary Poppins, an English nanny, has taken her two little charges, Jane and Michael, to a gingerbread shop owned by Mrs. Corry, a tiny, witchlike old woman with two large, sad daughters, Fannie and Annie. The following conversation develops:

"I suppose, my dear"—she turned to Mary Poppins, whom she appeared to know very well—"I suppose you've come for some gingerbread?"

"That's right, Mrs. Corry," said Mary Poppins politely.

"Good. Have Fannie and Annie given you any?" She looked at Jane and Michael as she said this.

"No, Mother," said Miss Fannie meekly.

"We were just going to, Mother—" began Miss Annie in a frightened whisper.

At that Mrs. Corry drew herself up to her full height and regarded her gigantic daughters furiously. Then she said in a soft, fierce, terrifying voice:

"Just going to? Oh, *indeed!* That is very interesting. And who, may I ask, Annie, gave you permission to give away my gingerbread—?"

"Nobody, Mother. And I didn't give it away. I only thought—"

"You only thought! That is *very* kind of you. But I will thank you not to think. *I* can do all the thinking that is necessary here!" said Mrs. Corry in her soft, terrible voice. Then she burst into a harsh cackle of laughter. "Look at her! Just look at her! Cowardy-custard! Crybaby!" she shrieked, pointing her knotty finger at her daughter.

Jane and Michael turned and saw a large tear coursing down Miss Annie's huge, sad face, and they did not like to say anything, for, in spite of her tininess, Mrs. Corry made them feel rather small and frightened. [172]

Within half a minute Mrs. Corry has managed to block poor Annie in all three areas of human functioning: acting, thinking and feeling. She first implies that to give the children some gingerbread would have been the right thing to do. When her daughters are about to apologize for not having done this yet, she suddenly denies their right to take that action. Annie tries to defend herself by pointing out that she did not actually do it, but only thought of doing it. Mrs. Corry promptly lets her know that she is not supposed to think. The way the mother expresses her displeasure leaves no doubt that this is an important matter and her daughter had better be sorry about what happened. With this she manages to drive Annie to tears and then immediately ridicules her feelings.

Let us not make the mistake of shrugging off this story because it is fiction, and children's fiction to boot. Research into the communication styles of families with a member who has been diagnosed as psychiatrically disturbed or into larger human conflicts shows that this pattern appears very frequently [13, 80, 82, 166, 167, 168, 174, 185]. It is called a double bind. What a double bind and the earlier examples have in common is that they are all structured like the paradoxes, or antinomies, in formal logic. But while for most of us formal paradoxes are merely amusing recollections from our school days, the paradoxes contained in communication are of stark practical importance. Very much as in the Mary Poppins story, there are three basic variations of the paradoxical theme:

1. If an individual is punished for correct perception of the outside world or of himself by a significant other (e.g., a child by a parent), he will learn to distrust the data of his senses. A predicament of this kind arises when, say, an alcoholic father demands that his children see him as a gentle, loving parent, even or especially when he comes home drunk and threatens them all with violence. The children are then forced to perceive reality not as it looks to them, but as their father defines it for them. A person who has repeatedly been exposed to this kind of confusion will find it very difficult to behave appropriately in many life situations and may spend inordinate amounts of time trying to find out how he "should" see reality. Examined out of its interpersonal context, his behavior would satisfy the diagnostic criteria of schizophrenia.

2. If an individual is expected by a significant other to have feelings different from those he actually experiences, he will eventually feel guilty for being unable to feel what he is told he ought to feel in order to be approved of by the other person. This guilt may itself be labeled one of the feelings he should not have. A dilemma of this kind arises

most frequently when a child's occasional normal sadness (or disappointment or fatigue) is construed by a parent as a silent imputation of parental failure. The parent typically reacts with the message "After all we have done for you, you ought to be happy." Sadness thus becomes associated with badness and ingratitude. In his fruitless attempts not to feel unhappy, the child displays behavior which, examined out of context, satisfies the diagnostic criteria of depression. Depression also occurs when an individual feels, or is held, responsible for something over which he has no control (e.g., marital conflict between his parents, the illness or failure of a parent or sibling, or his own inability to meet parental expectations that exceed his physical and/or emotional resources).

3. If a significant other gives injunctions that both demand and prohibit certain actions, a paradoxical situation arises in which the individual (again, notably a child) can obey only by disobeying. The prototype of this is: "Do what I say, not what I would like you to do." This is the message given by a mother who wants her teen-age son to be both law-abiding and a daredevil. The likely result is behavior that, examined out of context, satisfies the social definition of delinquency. Other examples are parents who place great value on winning by any means, fair or foul, but tell the child that "one should always be honest"; or a mother who begins to warn her daughter at a very early age of the dangers and ugliness of sex, but insists that she be "popular" with boys [180].

There is a fourth variation of this theme, and it is probably the most frequent in human interaction. It occurs whenever somebody demands of another person behavior that by its very nature must be spontaneous but now cannot be because it has been demanded. "Be spontaneous" paradoxes, as they are called, range in intensity from mild nuisances to tragic traps, depending on the importance of the need expressed through them. It is one of the shortcomings of human communication that there is no way in which the spontaneous fulfillment of a need can be elicited from another person without creating this kind of self-defeating paradox. A wife who needs a sign of affection from her husband eventually tells him, "I wish you would sometimes bring me flowers." The request is quite understandable, but by making it, she has irreversibly ruined her chances of getting what she wants: if her husband disregards her request, she will feel dissatisfied; if he now brings her flowers, she will also be dissatisfied, because he did not do it of his own accord.

Very much the same impasse arises between a child and his parents when they think he is not assertive enough. In one way or another they signal: "Don't be so obedient." Again this leaves only two alternatives, both unacceptable: either the child remains unassertive (in which case the parents will be dissatisfied because he is not obeying them) or he becomes more assertive (in which case they will be discontent because he is doing the right thing for the wrong reason—that is, he is obeying them). A person in this situation cannot win, but neither can the originator of the paradoxical request.

(A variation of the "Be spontaneous" theme, or rather its converse, considered a "nice touch" by certain hotel managers, is shown on the opposite page. Not only is the welcome expressed by the lapel button disqualified [contradicted] by the waitress's facial expression, but the statement itself, "We're glad you're here," is further disqualified by the way it is communicated. A welcome is meaningful only if it is given individually and spontaneously. But as a written message, worn by every employee of the hotel as part of the uniform, it is not simply meaningless, it gives the guest a good idea of the kind of "personalized" service he can expect. Here the paradox is contained not in a *demand* for spontaneous behavior, but in the indiscriminate, blanket *offer* of such behavior.)

The "Be spontaneous" pattern is a universal paradox. As recent advances in logic, especially in the computer sciences but also in pure mathematics, have shown, many seemingly unambiguous concepts are ultimately paradoxical (e.g., computability, provability, consistency, probability). The same holds true for more general concepts, such as spontaneity, trust, sanity or even power.

Power can indeed create its own paradoxes and double binds, as illustrated by an article called "The Japanese Hamlet," a study of the relationship between the United States and Japan in the mid-sixties. The author, Peter Schmid, a German journalist known for his analyses of international relations, saw Japan as a Hamlet torn between the mutually exclusive ideas of security and goodness:

> Power, the argument runs, is evil: therefore I renounce it—not entirely but as far as possible. A friend protects me. He is powerful . . . and therefore evil. . . . I despise, I hate

him for it, and yet I must stretch out my hand to him. I am powerless because I would like to be good . . . therefore my evil friend has power over me. I condemn what he, the powerful, does, and yet I tremble at the thought that he might stumble. For if my protector stumbles, as behooves the evil, then I, the good, will also stumble. [159]

Power, Lord Acton said, tends to corrupt, and absolute power corrupts absolutely. It is easy to see the evil effects of power; it is much harder to recognize the paradoxical consequences that come about when the existence of power is denied. The idea of a society free from power and coercion is an age-old utopian dream which is at present undergoing one of its periodic revivals. Contemporary idealists have rediscovered Rousseau's concept of the basically good natural man who is corrupted by society. It apparently matters little to them that today, as in Rousseau's time, this thesis fails to explain how the sum total of natural men manage to turn into the dark sinister power that is responsible for oppression, mental illness, suicide, divorce, alcoholism and crime. They continue to insist that mankind can and must be led back to the blissful state of total freedom, if necessary by force. But as Karl Popper warned in his famous 1945 treatise on *The Open Society and Its Enemies*, the paradise of the happy, primitive society (which, by the way, never really existed) is forever closed to those who have tasted the fruit of the tree of knowledge: "The more we try to return to the heroic age of tribalism, the more surely do we arrive at the Inquisition, the Secret Police, at a romanticized gangsterism" [135].

To put this paradox in a more concrete framework, great efforts are made in modern psychiatric hospitals to avoid any semblance of power in the relations between doctors, staff and patients. The goal of the treatment is the return of the patient to normalcy—a goal he cannot reach himself or he would not have had to be hospitalized. But no matter how much one may want to define normalcy in medical, psychological or philosophic terms, in practice it refers to very specific norms of behavior, which must be complied with spontaneously and not because the patient has no other choice. Herein lies the paradox: as long as the patient has to be helped to behave appropriately, he is a patient. It does not take much to show up the make-believe of noncoercion, spontaneity and equality. For example, during a ward picnic at a mental hospital recently, a patient was broiling steaks. A doctor came over and started a conversation with him while under their very eyes the steaks turned black. When the incident was discussed later, it turned out that the patient felt the doctor could and should have done something about the steaks if they were equals, while the psychiatrist had decided that he should not save the steaks because this would have communicated to the patient that he did not consider him capable of broiling them.

The most far-reaching attempt to create a truly coercion-free environment in our society is the so-called blow-out center, a small, residential treatment unit in which severely disturbed patients are cared for by dedicated helpers in a supposedly completely permissive milieu. But, of course, not even these centers can dispense altogether with a structure of power and, sometimes, very rigid rules with regard to certain behavior, such as violence toward others, sexual acting-out, drug abuse and suicide attempts. There would be absolutely nothing wrong with these restrictions if they were not imposed in a context of allegedly complete freedom from power and coercion. But the claim of noncoercion, which must be maintained at all costs, necessitates strange, almost schizophrenic denials of the obvious and renders these places more like home to the patients than the therapists care to think. It must be added that an inmate who, for example, is in the habit of yielding to some strong inner urge to smash all the windows on a cold winter night will eventually be forced to leave the home and thus again be placed at the mercy of the society that allegedly ruined him in the first place.[*]

Unfortunately, it is far more difficult to solve paradoxical situations than to diagnose the confusion created by them, largely because their resolution involves non-common sense and absurd or even seemingly dishonest actions, as two famous examples from history show.

Charles V ruled over an empire in which the sun did not set. This created fantastic communications problems for the officials of the Crown in the remote overseas possessions. They were supposed to carry out faithfully the imperial orders reaching them from Madrid, but often they could not, because the directives either were issued in crass ignorance of the local situation or arrived weeks if not months after being decreed, by which time they were largely obsolete. In Central America this dilemma led to a very pragmatic solution: *Se obedece pero no se cumple* (One obeys but does not comply). Thanks to this recipe, the Central American possessions flourished, not because but in spite of the imperial orders from the Escorial. Two centuries later this expedient was awarded official recognition under the reign of Empress Maria Theresa through the establishment of the Order of Maria Theresa. It remained Austria's highest military decoration until the end of World War I (and in the face of all logic, Hungary's even well into World War II). With refreshing absurdity it was reserved exclusively for officers who turned the tide of battle by taking matters into their own hands and actively disobeying orders.

---

[*] Rémy de Gourmont must have had a similar paradox in mind when he wrote: *"Quand la morale triomphe, il se passe des choses très vilaines"* (When morals triumph, many very evil things happen).

Of course, if things went wrong, they were not decorated but court-martialed for disobedience. The Order of Maria Theresa is perhaps the supreme example of an official counterparadox, worthy of a nation whose attitude toward the slings and arrows of outrageous fortune has always been characterized by the motto: The situation is hopeless but not serious.

A structurally similar but more untenable paradox is found in Joseph Heller's novel *Catch-22* [66]. Yossarian, a World War II pilot with a U.S. bomber squadron in the Mediterranean, feels that he is beginning to lose his mind under the inhuman stress of the daily combat missions. Short of being killed in action, the only way out is to be grounded for psychiatric reasons. He begins to explore this possibility with the flight surgeon, Dr. Daneeka, and learns that this is perfectly possible. All he has to do is ask to be grounded. Yossarian, an old hand at military logic, cannot quite believe the simplicity of this solution, and on further inquiry Dr. Daneeka tells him the whole truth: there is one catch, and that is a regulation called Catch-22, based on the undeniable fact that to fear for one's life in a dangerous situation is a perfectly normal reaction. Therefore, anybody willing to fly combat missions would have to be crazy, and being crazy, could be grounded for psychiatric reasons. He has only to ask to be. But the very process of asking, of not wanting to fly any more combat missions, is evidence of normalcy and rules out being grounded for psychiatric reasons. Thus, anybody who flew combat missions was really insane and could therefore be grounded; but if he did not want to fly them, he was reacting appropriately, normally, and had no excuse for not flying them.

The world of war and any world that utilizes totalitarian violence is itself insane, and in it, sanity becomes a manifestation of madness or badness. Whether the scene is the cockpit of a bomber or a "people's court" dispensing the most reactionary or the most revolutionary justice, human values and the laws of communication are turned upside down and the darkness of confusion falls upon victims and victimizers alike.

3

The Benefits of Confusion

It might seem that there is nothing good about confusion, but this is not quite the case. Suppose everybody starts laughing as I enter a room. This is very confusing to me because the others either see the reality of the situation very differently than I do or are in possession of some information that I do not have. My immediate reaction is to search for clues—from looking to see if somebody is behind me to wondering if they have just been talking about me; from going to a mirror to see if I have a smudge on my face to demanding an explanation.

After the initial shock, confusion triggers off an immediate search for meaning or order to reduce the anxiety inherent in any uncertain situation. The result is an unusual increase in attention, coupled with a readiness to assume causal connections even where such connections may appear to be quite nonsensical. While the search can be extended to include such small details or such remote possibilities that it leads to further confusion, it can equally well lead to fresh and creative ways of conceptualizing reality.

Anybody who is confused is likely to jump to conclusions by holding on to the first apparently reliable piece of evidence that he detects through the fog of his confusion.° This, too, can be turned to positive advantage. The famous hypnotherapist Dr. Milton H. Erickson has developed it into a sophisticated therapeutic intervention called the Confusion Technique. He describes its discovery as follows:

> One windy day . . . a man came rushing around the corner of a building and bumped hard against me as I stood bracing myself against the wind. Before he could recover his poise to speak to me, I glanced elaborately at my watch and courteously, as if he had enquired the time of day, I stated, "It's exactly ten minutes of two," though it was actually closer to 4:00 P.M., and walked on. About half a block away,

---

° This may help to explain the often reported fact that the emotionally confusing state of one's first sexual excitement and climax may attach itself to some totally unrelated factor that happened to be co-present at the time, which can lead to odd sexual fixations and rituals. For instance, a man was reported to be capable of having an erection only when his partner pulled his ear, and this was traced back to his first successful act of masturbation, during which he was caught by the teacher and had his ear pulled. *Se non è vero, è ben trovato* (If it isn't true, it's well invented), the Italians say. The film *Casanova '70* spoofs this very mechanism: Marcello Mastroianni plays the role of the hero who can make love only if the situation is extremely dangerous or he has very little time. Unfortunately for him, fate leads him again and again into perfectly safe encounters with beautiful women who have all the time in the world, so he either becomes impotent or has to go to hilarious extremes to make the situation dangerous or urgent. A similar scene can be found in Woody Allen's film *Everything You Always Wanted to Know about Sex but Were Afraid to Ask.*

I turned and saw him still looking at me, undoubtedly still puzzled and bewildered by my remark. [39]

Erickson has shown that by creating a similar confusion through the use of vague, ambiguous and puzzling statements, the hypnotic subject is very likely to invest the first concrete, understandable piece of information he is given with an unusual degree of importance and validity. And since psychotherapy is fundamentally the art of changing a person's view of reality, Confusion Technique is a particularly powerful intervention. (Needless to say, in the hands of an unethical person it can be put to very negative ends.)

In other words, confusion sharpens our senses and our attention to detail. Under unusual circumstances, such as great danger, one functions in ways that may be very different from one's usual, everyday behavior. "In a split second" and "without thinking" one may make the right, lifesaving decision. The same thing also happens under less exceptional conditions, as a response to confusion. It happens most frequently when for one reason or another we go into a situation in an almost absent-minded mood. Absent-mindedness shares many of the positive effects of confusion. For instance, somebody in a hurry takes off his jacket and carelessly throws it in the general direction of a chair; much to his surprise it drapes itself neatly over the back. If he tries to repeat the feat, he fails—and he is left with the vague impression that his consciously willing himself to do it somehow caused his failure. There is a vast and interesting literature on the subject, especially Far Eastern texts. Both the Taoist concept of *wu-wei* ("deliberate inattention") and the Zen teachings of letting go and freeing one's mind, described in Herrigel's beautiful little book on *Zen in the Art of Archery* [67] are a part of this.

I am not competent to judge whether any "higher" powers of the mind are involved in all of this, but there can be no doubt that a certain degree of conscious inattention enables us to be more receptive to the countless minimal, nonverbal clues inherent in all interactional situations, be they between humans or between humans and animals. Animals have indeed an extraordinary ability to perceive and interpret correctly very minimal clues, as the story of Clever Hans amply demonstrates.

The case of Clever Hans

In 1904 a wave of excitement swept through the scientific community of Europe; one of mankind's oldest and fondest dreams had come true—human communication had been established with an animal. The animal was Hans, an eight-year-old stallion belonging to a retired Berlin schoolteacher, Wilhelm von Osten. Judging from contemporary accounts [e.g., 32, 169], the excitement spread from the most respected and sober-minded scientists of the time to the general public. Zoologists, psychologists, physicians, neuropsychiatrists, physiologists, veterinarians, entire panels of experts and academic committees, formed expressly for the purpose, made pilgrimages to the prosaic cobblestone courtyard in a northern suburb of the city where Clever Hans, as he came to be known, had his stable and gave his amazing performances. Many of these visitors went full of skepticism, but apparently they all left fully convinced and literally awed by what they had seen.

What von Osten, with an obviously boundless belief in his profession,° had achieved was to turn his pedagogic talents

---

° In his introduction of a book on the case [126], Professor Carl Stumpf described von Osten as follows:

A former instructor of mathematics in a German gymnasium, a passionate horseman and hunter, extremely patient and at the same from little brats to his beautiful horse and to teach him not only arithmetic but such additional feats as telling time, recognizing photographs of people he had met, and many other, unbelievable abilities [125].

Clever Hans communicated his answers by tapping his hoof. Nonnumerical answers he tapped out in German, letter by letter; he had been taught the alphabet and to give one tap for the letter *a*, two for *b*, and so on. He was put to extremely careful scientific tests, designed to eliminate even the remotest possibility of some sort of secret signaling by his master. But he passed them all with flying colors, especially since he did almost as well in von Osten's absence as in his presence. On September 12, 1904, a panel composed of thirteen scientists and experts, some of them members of the Prussian Academy of Science, others professors from the University of Berlin, published a report which ruled out deception or unintentional signaling and accorded the highest scientific importance and respectability to this remarkable horse.

Barely three months later, another report was published. Its author was Professor Carl Stumpf, one of the members of the September commission. He had continued to study the strange horse. Apparently it was Oskar Pfungst, one of his assistants (he later wrote a book on the subject [124]), who could not reconcile himself to the touching idea of a horse genius and made the decisive discovery. But Pfungst was only a *cand.phil. et med.* (a graduate student in philosophy

---

time highly irascible, liberal in permitting the use of the horse for days at a time and again tyrannical in the insistence upon foolish conditions, clever in his method of instruction and yet at the same time possessing not even the slightest notion of the most elementary conditions of scientific procedure—all this, and more, goes to make up the man. He is fanatic in his conviction, he has an eccentric mind which is crammed full of theories from the phrenology of Gall to the belief that the horse is capable of inner speech.

and medicine), and in good academic tradition the report's official author was Stumpf. Pfungst's discovery, to quote from the report, was that

> the horse failed in his responses whenever the solution of the problem that was given him was unknown to any of those present. For instance, when a written number or the objects to be counted were placed before the horse, but were invisible to everyone else, and especially to the questioner, he failed to respond properly. Therefore he can neither count, nor read, nor solve problems in arithmetic.
>
> The horse failed again whenever he was prevented by means of sufficiently large blinders from seeing the persons, and especially the questioner, to whom the solution was known. He therefore required some sort of visual aid.
>
> These aids need not, however—and this is the peculiarly interesting feature in the case—be given intentionally. [127]

The report goes on to explain:

> So far as I can see, the following explanation is the only one that will comport with these facts. The horse must have learned, in the course of the long period of problem-solving, to attend ever more closely, while tapping, to the slight changes in bodily posture with which the master unconsciously accompanied the steps in his own thought-processes, and to use these as closing signals. The motive for this direction and straining of attention was the regular reward in the form of carrots and bread, which attended it. This unexpected kind of independent activity and the certainty and precision of the perception of minimal movements thus attained, are astounding in the highest degree.
>
> The movements which call forth the horse's reaction are so extremely slight in the case of Mr. von Osten, that it is easily comprehensible how it was possible that they should escape the notice even of practised observers. Mr. Pfungst, however, whose previous laboratory experience had made

him keen in the perception of visual stimuli of slightest duration and extent, succeeded in recognizing in Mr. von Osten the different kinds of movements which were the basis of the various accomplishments of the horse. Furthermore, he succeeded in controlling his own movements (of which he had hitherto been unconscious), in the presence of the horse, and finally became so proficient that he could replace these unintentional movements by intentional ones. He can now call forth at will all the various reactions of the horse by making the proper kind of voluntary movements, without asking the relevant question or giving any sort of command. But Mr. Pfungst meets with the same success when he does not attend to the movements to be made, but rather focuses, as intently as possible, upon the number desired, since in that case the necessary movement occurs whether he wills it or not. [128]

As can be imagined, von Osten (whose honesty was never in question) was deeply upset by these findings. At first, his anger turned against Clever Hans, in a way that Pfungst describes as tragicomic, but soon afterward he believed his horse again and permitted no further investigations. In typical human fashion he opted for a view of reality in accordance with his beliefs rather than with undeniable facts—a subject that will occupy us again in the second part of this book.

The Clever Hans trauma

By the time Pfungst's discovery became generally known, other gifted horses with similar or even greater abilities had been discovered in Elbersfeld. There were also talking (barking) dogs in Mannheim and various other animals, including pigs, which had learned to carry out fantastically complicated computations and in their spare time startled

their human interviewers with witty or philosophical remarks.

The harsh truth of Pfungst's results shattered all this, and
the pendulum swung to the other extreme, an extreme from
which ethology (the modern name for animal psychology)
has not yet recovered. Professor H. Hediger, the former
director of the Zurich zoo, has written an excellent paper on
this trauma, summarizing its effect as follows:

> It is evident that from this entire movement involving
> tap-communicating animals which, after all, lasted for more
> than a quarter century and produced world-wide contro-
> versy and an enormous literature, that from this gigantic
> lapsus only negative consequences have so far been drawn:
> the avoidance of the Clever Hans mistake by absolutely
> preventing any involuntary signalling—which practically
> means: by the strict elimination of any direct contact
> between animal and man in psychological experiments with
> animals. [64]

But, as Hediger observes, this throws the baby out with
the bath water; no attention is now paid either to the
fantastic ability of animals to perceive and interpret correctly muscular (especially mimic) movements as small as
$\frac{1}{5}$ mm (a fact that Pfungst verified experimentally in his
work with Clever Hans), or to the fact that we humans
constantly emit signals of which we are unaware and over
which we have no control. "For the animal," Hediger states,
"we are often transparent to a (for us) unpleasant degree.
Strangely enough, this realization, which in a certain sense
is embarrassing, has so far been only the object of repres-
sion, but never the starting point of research into more
intensive modes of comprehension and communication"
[65].

Although officially ignored, these signals are the subject of many charming and astonishing episodes between animals and between men and animals. That animals should be experts in reading and interpreting minimal clues is not too surprising. In their daily lives they are constantly faced with situations in which survival depends on split-second evaluation and decision making. You are a monkey, the primate researcher Ray Carpenter once explained to the anthropologist Robert Ardrey,

and you're running along a path past a rock and unexpectedly meet face to face another animal. Now, before you know whether to attack it, to flee it, or to ignore it, you must make a series of decisions. Is it monkey or non-monkey? If non-monkey, is it pro-monkey or anti-monkey? If monkey, is it male or female? If female, is she interested? If male, is it adult or juvenile? If adult, is it of my group or some other? If it is of my group, then what is its rank, above or below me? You have about one fifth of a second to make all these decisions, or you could be attacked. [8]

Anybody who maintains a close relationship with an animal, especially a cat, dog or horse, knows how incredibly perceptive that animal can be when it comes to affect-laden issues; that is, to those issues that make humans drop some of their intellectual attitudes and thus become more spontaneous and understandable to animals. Hediger refers to an account of the bear mascot of a British artillery unit who in a combat situation during World War II, without being trained to do so, spontaneously picked up a 15-mm shell and fell in with the ammunition carriers [57].

Another charming, allegedly true story is "The Bear That Came for Supper," by Robert F. Leslie [87], a Texan who likes to spend his vacations climbing mountains, fishing and canoeing. One afternoon, while fishing in the wilderness of western Canada, he was approached by a huge black bear.

Since he was alone and unarmed, he had every reason to try to convince the bear of his friendly feelings, hoping for a lifesaving degree of sympathy in return. It was clearly a situation in which reason and intellect were of precious little help, because there was no past experience to provide a guideline. In this typical example of creative confusion, unimpeded by useless thinking, he fed the bear every trout he caught, and the bear became quite chummy, half leaning against him as they both sat on the riverbank. Gradually, over the course of several days, a most extraordinary relationship developed, based mostly on the bear's needs and whims and his growing confidence that the human could and would satisfy them. Hediger, who had an extensive correspondence with Leslie about all details of this unusual story, considers it a true account, especially in the light of many other, similar reports of bear behavior.

Subtle power

One researcher who managed to remain unaffected by the Clever Hans trauma, but fully recognized the importance of studying the minimal clues going back and forth between experimenters and their subjects, was the psychologist Robert Rosenthal, who edited the English edition of the Clever Hans story. His name is linked to experiments at Harvard University which show to what an astonishing extent the tacit assumptions and biases of an experimenter can influence the performance of rats, even when the experimenter is fully convinced that he is keeping his bias out [145].

Rosenthal also studied the effect of intentional but concealed biasing of human beings. Subjects were shown photographs of people and asked to use whatever criteria they felt useful in judging the degree of success (on a scale ranging from − 10 for "very unsuccessful" to + 10 for "very successful") these people had achieved in their lives. (The pictures were of publicly unknown people, and in a series of standardization tests with many subjects, had been found to evoke predominantly "zero" responses.) A random rating along the scale from − 10 to + 10 was arbitrarily assigned to each experimenter, who was instructed somehow to influence his subjects in such a way that they would rate these pictures as closely to the arbitrarily assigned value as possible. The experiments were filmed and shown to a large group of observers who knew what the experiment was about but did not know the number the experimenter was trying to make his subjects choose. The observers' task was to guess this number by watching the film. As Rosenthal reports, the accuracy of their guesses made it clear that the ratings each experimenter was trying to make his subjects choose (without ever directly referring to them) were equally accessible to the observers.

We thus see again that in situations in which our usual perceptive and intellectual capabilities are no longer able to supply the answers, we avail ourselves of certain other capabilities that do not appear to be under conscious control but are apparently activated by the puzzling and confusing aspects of the situation. Rosenthal's work leaves little doubt that we are all at the mercy of influences of which we are unaware and over which we have virtually no conscious control. What is even more frightening is that we ourselves, no matter how careful and discreet we believe ourselves to be, are constantly influencing others in ways of which we may be only dimly or not at all aware. Indeed, we may unconsciously be responsible for influences of which we consciously know nothing and which, if we knew them, we might find totally unacceptable.

This is particularly apparent in family interaction. For instance, in the examples of double-binding in families mentioned on pages 18–20, half of the paradoxical message is often given nonverbally and covertly, as in the case of the mother of a juvenile delinquent who displays two very different attitudes toward her offspring: an "official," punitive, censoring one, which verbally demands good behavior and respect for society's rules; and a nonverbal, seductive one, of which she may honestly be unaware, but which is very noticeable to the outside observer and especially to the delinquent, who is only too alert to the gleam in her eye and her secret admiration for his questionable exploits. In a very similar fashion, a therapist may quite unwittingly add to the problem of his patient if for one reason or another he feels hopeless about or repelled by it. This is apt to happen if the problem is one that he himself is unable to solve in his own private life, like drinking. He may then *talk* in a positive manner but covertly affect his patient in a very negative way. (Similarly, a therapist's professional fears may bring about the feared outcome, as reflected in the old *bon mot* about hypnotherapy: The effects of hypnosis can be dangerous if the therapist believes that the effects of hypnosis can be dangerous.)

When Rosenthal and others began to publish their findings in this field, a great deal of controversy arose over the question of how these subtle yet powerful clues are transmitted. It is one thing to influence someone's opinions in a general way; to elicit from him as concrete a response as a supposedly independent rating between -10 and $+10$ is a very different matter.

Meanwhile another piece of highly imaginative and novel research in this area, carried out by Eckhard H. Hess at the University of Chicago, provided some partial answers. Hess was led into this work by a chance event:

> One night about five years ago, I was lying in bed leafing through a book of strikingly beautiful animal photographs.

My wife happened to glance over at me and remarked that the light must be bad—my pupils were unusually large. It seemed to me that there was plenty of light coming from the bedside lamp and said so, but she insisted that my pupils were dilated. [68]

In subsequent experiments, prompted by this incident, Hess discovered that pupil size is by no means determined only by the intensity of the light falling into the eyes (as is sometimes assumed), but also very much by emotional factors.

As is often the case, writers seem to have known this for a long time: "his eyes narrowed with hate," "her eyes brimmed with love." But it remained for Hess to show that such expressions were more than poetic images. He found that magicians often watch for sudden changes in pupil size; when the card a person has been thinking about is turned up, his pupils are likely to enlarge. Chinese jade dealers watch for the same reaction in a potential buyer's eyes and thus get a good idea of which piece of jewelry he likes and may be willing to pay a high price for.

One of Hess's experiments consisted in showing his subjects two photographs of an attractive young woman's face. They were printed from the same negative and therefore identical, except that the pupils of one photo had been retouched to make them extra large. The average response to that picture, writes Hess,

was more than twice as strong as the response to the one with small pupils; nevertheless, when the men were questioned after the experimental session, most of them reported that the two pictures were identical. Some did say that one was "more feminine" or "prettier" or "softer." None noticed that one had larger pupils than the other. In fact, they had to be shown the difference. As long ago as the Middle Ages women dilated their pupils with the drug belladonna (which means "beautiful woman" in Italian). Clearly large pupils are attractive to men, but the response to them—at least in our subjects—is apparently at a nonverbal level. One might hazard a guess that what is appealing about large pupils in a woman is that they imply extraordinary interest in the man she is with! [69]

Research into these extremely subtle channels of communication has so far only scratched the surface of an undoubtedly very fertile field, but we already know that pupil size is only one of many modes of nonverbal communication based on specific body reactions, and involving not only seeing and hearing but also smell and touch.

"Extrasensory perception"

All of this points in one direction: we are far more perceptive and far more influenced by our perceptions than we think we are—in other words, we are constantly engaged in the give and take of a communication of which we know nothing, but which does much to determine our behavior.[*] The reader who is so inclined could easily set up a Rhine-type experiment in which just about anybody can be made into an extrasensory perception (ESP) expert. These experiments use a deck of cards with five symbols— cross, circle, square, pentagram or wavy lines. The experimenter looks at one card after another, making sure that the subject cannot see them, and the subject is supposed to guess, through ESP, which of the five symbols the experimenter is looking at. There is one guess per card, and after every guess the experimenter tells the subject whether he

[*] There is a good deal of literature on behavior without awareness, and part of it was well summarized in a journal article by Joe Adams in 1957 [5].

was right or wrong. This is again one of those situations in which the apparent impossibility of the task produces that creative confusion in which most of us fall back on our most subtle perceptions—presumably out of sheer desperation. If the experimenter were to give some minimal clue as he looks at a certain symbol, or if a certain faint noise were always produced just then in, say, an adjoining room, the subject's "ESP" curve would rise steeply and his success rate would approach 100 percent, provided, of course, that the same minimal clue was always given for the same symbol. Needless to say, a lot of fraudulent hocus-pocus could be achieved in this way, but what is really interesting about it is the fact that this kind of signaling is so amazingly successful, although—or precisely because—it remains completely outside the subject's awareness. In all probability a lot of face-to-face mind reading and clairvoyance is based on some people's natural perceptivity to these minimal clues.

Long before behavioral scientists became aware of these phenomena, Edgar Allan Poe had made this ability the basis of "The Murders in the Rue Morgue." The narrator of the story and his friend Dupin, who is described as an unusually keen observer of even the most trifling facts and events, are strolling through Paris. Suddenly Dupin says, "He is a very little fellow, that's true, and would do better for the *Théâtre des Variétés*." The other is dumbfounded. "Dupin," he says gravely,

this is beyond my comprehension. I do not hesitate to say that I am amazed, and can scarcely credit my senses. How was it you should know I was thinking of—?" Here I paused, to ascertain beyond a doubt whether he really knew of whom I thought. "—of Chantilly," said he, "why do you pause? You were remarking to yourself that his diminutive figure unfitted him for tragedy."

This was precisely what had formed the subject of my reflections. Chantilly was a *quondam* cobbler of the Rue St.

Denis, who, becoming stage-mad, had attempted the *rôle* of Xerxes, in Crébillon's tragedy so called, and been notoriously Pasquinaded for his pains.

"Tell me, for Heaven's sake," I exclaimed, "the method—if method there is—by which you have been enabled to fathom my soul in this matter."

And through the mouth of Dupin, Poe gives a scientifically convincing reconstruction of the events experienced by the two men during the past fifteen minutes, anticipating such then-unknown concepts as free association, nonverbal communication and other behavior analyses that make this totally fictional reconstruction read like a piece of modern behavior research.

Before concluding this section on the benefits of confusion, a brief remark on the only funny side of so dead-serious a subject as psychoanalysis seems in order. As is well known, the psychoanalytic patient is made to lie on a couch and is supposed to practice a special form of mental confusion called free association, that is, to say anything and everything that comes to his mind. The analyst sits behind him, out of the patient's sight. The official reason for this arrangement is that it facilitates the free flow of the associations, especially the more embarrassing ones, by making the patient less aware of the analyst's presence. But, to use a psychoanalytic analogy, what is thrown out the front door sneaks in the rear: far from forgetting the analyst's presence, the patient develops an especially keen sense for minimal accoustical clues coming from behind him. The scratching of the doctor's pen, the squeaking of his chair, the almost imperceptible sound of his stroking his beard, all these gradually develop into highly significant messages telling the patient what he is supposed to free-associate and what not, until a certain type of rhythmic breathing informs him that his therapist has finally dozed off.

PART II
Disinformation

4

Noncontingency, or the Emergence of World Views

Order is heav'n's first law.

—Alexander Pope

It is the theory which decides what we can observe.

—Albert Einstein

We have so far looked at situations in which the meaning of a message did not "get through," either because something happened to it in the course of its transmission (and/or translation), or because the message itself was so structured that it contradicted (disqualified) itself and created a paradox. In either case the outcome was confusion, which, by producing uncertainty, provides a powerful stimulus to the quest for structure and order.

We will now see how states of uncertainty can be produced not by ineptitude, default or paradox, but experimentally, so that it becomes possible to study how organisms behave as they try to relieve uncertainty.

We will turn next to real-life situations, predicaments in which the "experimenter" is no longer human but conceived of as some rather vague concept of order which, depending on the reader's philosophical preference, may be called reality, nature, fate or God. The epigrams by Pope and Einstein above are meant to forewarn him of how contradictory the results of this search for order may be.

This will lead to contexts in which, on the one hand, communication between two partners is somehow physically impossible but in which, on the other hand, a joint decision *must* be reached. Finally, we will consider the problems of actively withholding true and supplying false information, as in the case of counterespionage and especially double-agent work.

Whether these communication impasses are experimentally produced, inherent in certain concrete obstacles or deliberately created, they have a common denominator for which I have adopted the intelligence term of *disinformation*. Its meaning should become understandable in what follows.

There is a whole class of experiments designed to test and study the ways in which animal or human subjects go about finding or introducing order when faced with a context of disinformation. What these experiments all have in common is that they require the subject to use the utmost ingenuity to find an order in what actually has no order at all. This leads to results of great psychiatric and philosophic interest. They differ from the much better known learning experiments in that there is no connection whatever between a subject's performance and the reward or punishment that he receives, but he does not know this. He believes that if he manages to respond "correctly," he will be rewarded, and if he fails, he will be punished—or, in other words, that the reaction he gets is contingent upon his performance. In actual fact it is not, hence the term *noncontingent reward* experiments.

Here are some examples of experimentally produced disinformation, in ascending order of complexity:

The neurotic horse

If a horse receives a mild electric shock from a metal plate on the floor of its stall every time a bell rings, it will very soon come to associate the bell with the imminent shock and lift its hoof to avoid it. Once this conditioned reflex has been established, the shock mechanism can be turned off, and the horse will continue to lift its hoof whenever the bell rings. And every time it does this, the "success" of the action, i.e., the nonoccurrence of the shock, further convinces it that lifting its hoof is the "right" reaction. It never learns that the bell is no longer followed by a shock. For all practical purposes, it has acquired a neurotic symptom, persisting in an action that once was appropriate but no longer is. And, it need hardly be said, this kind of problem is by no means limited to animals [181].

The superstitious rat

Superstition is usually considered a purely human affliction through which we hope to establish some order in, and gain some control over, the capricious uncertainty of the world around us. But it can fairly easily be produced in animals, such as the laboratory rat (as well as in pigeons [115, 165]). A rat is released from its cage into an area about three feet long with a food tray on the far side. Ten seconds after the rat's arrival, food is dropped into the tray. If the rat gets to the tray *less* than ten seconds after its release, it gets no food. Before long the rat, with its practical mind, manages "to put two and two together." Since it takes the rat only two seconds to run directly to the food tray, the extra time has to be spent in a way that is basically alien to the rat's normal inclination to head straight for food. Under these circumstances the delay acquires a pseudocausal significance; whatever the rat does during these eight seconds becomes, in the rat's eyes, the "necessary" action that "produces," or is "rewarded" by, the appearance of food. These behavior patterns, of course, vary from rat to rat, which gives them a particularly capricious aspect: back-and-forth movements, a certain number of pirouettes to the right or the left, jumps (which the rat may have done purely accidentally at first), are faithfully repeated time after time. And every time the rat finds food in the tray, its belief is confirmed that this particular behavior is what produces the food. These types of behavior are the obvious equivalent of compulsive human superstitions, which are often based on the vague belief that they are required by some "divine experimenter."

The more complicated, the better

Professor Alex Bavelas, a noted expert in small-group interaction, has shown in several experiments that this kind of disinformation has a powerful influence on a human being's sense of reality.

In one experiment, two subjects, A and B, are seated facing a projection screen. There is a partition between them so that they cannot see each other, and they are requested not to communicate. They are then shown medical slides of healthy and sick cells and told that they must learn to recognize which is which by trial and error. In front of each of them are two buttons marked "Healthy" and "Sick," respectively, and two signal lights marked "Right" and "Wrong." Every time a slide is projected they have to press one of the buttons, whereupon one of the two signal lights flashes on.

A gets true feedback; that is, the lights tell him whether his guess was indeed right or wrong. His situation is one of simple discrimination, and in the course of the experiment, most A subjects learn to distinguish healthy from sick cells with a fair degree of correctness (i.e., about 80 percent of the time).

B's situation is very different. His feedback is based not on his own guesses, but on A's. Therefore it does not matter what he decides about a particular slide; he is told "right" if A guessed right, "wrong" if A guessed wrong. B does not know this; he has been led to believe there is an order, that he has to discover this order, and that he can do so by making guesses and finding out if he was right or wrong. But as he asks the "sphinx" he gets very confusing answers because he does not know that the sphinx is not talking to *him*. In other words, there is no way in which he can discover that the answers he gets are noncontingent—that is, have nothing to do with his questions—and that therefore he is not learning anything about his guesses. So he is searching for an order where there is none that *he* could discover.

A and B are eventually asked to discuss what they have come to consider the rules for distinguishing between healthy and sick cells. A's explanations are simple and concrete; B's are of necessity very subtle and complex—after all, he had to form his hypothesis on the basis of very tenuous and contradictory hunches.

The amazing thing is that A does not simply shrug off B's explanations as unnecessarily complicated or even absurd, but is impressed by their sophisticated "brilliance." A tends to feel inferior and vulnerable because of the pedestrian simplicity of his assumption, and the more complicated B's "delusions," the more likely they are to convince A. (This contagiousness of delusions is only too well known outside the communication researcher's laboratory, and we shall later consider some glaring examples.)

Before they take a second, identical test (but with new slides), A and B are asked to guess who will now do better than in his first test. All Bs and most As say that B will. In actual fact, B shows hardly any improvement, but comparatively speaking, seems to be doing better because A, who now shares at least some of B's abstruse ideas, performs significantly more poorly than the first time [18].

What Bavelas' ingenious experiment teaches us has far-reaching consequences: it shows that once a tentative explanation has taken hold of our minds, information to the contrary may produce not corrections but *elaborations* of the explanation. This means that the explanation becomes "self-sealing"; it is a conjecture that cannot be refuted.° But as Popper [133] has shown, refutability is the *conditio sine qua non* of scientific explanation. Conjectures of the kind we are considering here are thus pseudoscientific, superstitious, and ultimately, in a very real sense, psychotic. As we look at world history, we find that similarly "irrefutable" conjectures have been responsible for the worst atrocities.

° Armed with the peculiar logic of a self-sealing premise, one arrives at an ultimate certainty of sorts. If the premise is that prayer can heal illness, then a patient's death "proves" that he lacked faith, which in turn "proves" the correctness of the premise. In a similar vein, Lenin Prize-winner Sergey Mikhalkov matter-of-factly explained in a recent interview, "No convinced Communist can turn anti-Communist. Solzhenitsyn never was a Communist" [101]. In a controversy over the claim that behavior therapy is a quick and reliable treatment of phobias, the spokesman for the psychoanalytic side summed things up by saying about a book on the behavior-therapy approach to phobias that the author "defines the condition in a way that is acceptable only to conditioning theorists and does not fulfill the criteria of the psychiatric definition of this disorder. Therefore, his statements should not apply to phobias, but to some other condition" [152]. The conclusion is inescapable: a phobia that can be cured by behavior therapy is *for this reason* no phobia.

The Inquisition, ideas of racial superiority, the claim of totalitarian ideologies to have found the ultimate answer, immediately come to mind as examples.

The multi-armed bandit

The difficulty of changing somebody's outlook, once such a conjecture makes him see the world in a particular way, is borne out by another experiment. The reader probably knows what a one-armed bandit is: a gambling machine in which three or four disks spin as the player pulls a lever (the "arm"). If two or more disks stop in the same position, the player wins; if (as is much more probable) they don't, the machine swallows the coin that was put in to unlock the arm. The player is thus playing against the capricious, unpredictable "behavior" of the machine, and it is not at all unusual for him to develop superstitions about the inner life of the one-armed bandit. (This is as harmless a delusion as the funny contortions a bowler makes *after* he has let go of the ball, contortions that apparently are supposed to correct the path of the ball as it speeds down the alley.)

A superficially similar but much more sophisticated machine was built by the psychologist John C. Wright, who called it the multi-armed bandit. Strictly speaking, it has no arms, but rather sixteen pushbuttons, arranged in a circle on a sloping panel. These are unmarked and indistinguishable from one another, except for their location. In the center of the circle there is a seventeenth button, identical to the others. Above the circle, on a vertical panel, is a three-digit counter (see drawing on page 52).

The subject is seated in front of this machine and given the following instructions:

This is an experiment in problem solving. Your task is to operate these buttons in such a way as to get the largest

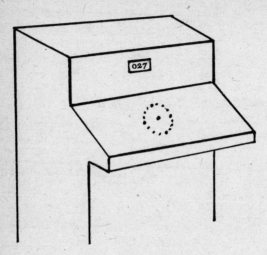

The multi-armed bandit

possible score up here on the counter. Of course, you will not know how to do this at first, and you will have to start by guessing, but you should be able to improve your guesses as you go along. Whenever you hit a correct button, or one of a correct sequence of buttons, you will hear a buzzer, and your score on the counter will go up by one point. You will never earn more than one point at a time and you will never lose any points.

You must begin by pressing any button on the perimeter of the circle once. Then press the center button to test whether or not you have just earned a point. If you have, you will hear the buzzer when you press the center test button. Then return to the perimeter and press a button (either the same one or a different one) and again test by pressing the center button. So every other time you press a button, it must be the center button.°

° Not only these instructions but the entire description of the experiment is presented here greatly abbreviated from [189] and [190].

What the subject does not know is that his "reward" (the buzzer, telling him that he has pressed the "right" button or buttons) is noncontingent; that is, there is no connection between his performance and the buzzer signals.

The experiment consists of an uninterrupted series of 325 button pushes (trials), subdivided into 13 blocks of 25 trials each. During the first 10 blocks (the first 250 trials) the subject receives a certain percentage of random rewards. During blocks 11 and 12 (the next 50 trials) he gets no rewards whatsoever; during block 13 (the last 25 button pushes) he is rewarded by the buzzer every single time.

Put yourself in the subject's place: after pressing some buttons unsuccessfully, the buzzer suddenly sounds for the first time. Since a condition of the experiment is that you are not allowed to keep a written record, you must try to reconstruct from memory exactly what you did right. You try again, but without success. At first there does not seem to be any rhyme or reason to the rewards. As you go along, some tentative rules seem to offer themselves. But then disaster strikes (blocks 11 and 12); suddenly nothing you do is right. Fortunately, just as all seems lost and hopeless, you hit upon a new idea and from then on (block 13) you are completely right: you have found the solution!

At this point, subjects are told the truth about the experimental setup. But they are at first unable to believe it. Some even assume that the experimenter is the deluded one, that they have discovered a regularity in the functioning of the device inside the machine that the experimenter never noticed. Others have to be actually shown the wiring of the apparatus before they believe the noncontingent nature of the experiment.°

° The anthropologist Gregory Bateson once wondered what a so-called schizophrenic would say in this situation, and decided that he would come to this conclusion: These buttons don't mean a thing—there is

This relatively simple experiment faithfully reproduces the essence of a universal human problem: once we have arrived at a solution—and in the process of getting there, have paid a fairly high price in terms of anxiety and expectation—our investment in this solution becomes so great that we may prefer to distort reality to fit our solution rather than sacrifice the solution.

Wright was able to show that the most elaborate delusions about the "right" way of pressing the buttons were created when the subject was rewarded 50 percent of the time during blocks 1 to 10. Subjects who were rewarded at a rate higher than 50 percent developed rather simple theories; those who were rewarded at a much lower rate tended to consider the task impossible and perhaps gave up. Again, the parallelism with real life is evident—and disturbing.

---

somebody in the other room who sounds the buzzer whenever he feels like it [17].

5
Randomness and Rules

"Nature abhors a vacuum," Spinoza quoted Cicero, and those of us who are not philosophers of science generally find it plausible that nature should somehow want to keep things tidy. But if we shuffled a deck of cards and then found that they had arranged themselves neatly into the four suits, each running from ace all the way up to king, we would consider this a little too tidy to be believable. When a statistician tells us that this outcome is exactly as probable as any other outcome, we do not quite understand him, until it finally dawns on us that, indeed, *any* order produced by shuffling is as probable or as improbable as the one just mentioned. This one seems unusual for reasons that have nothing to do with probability but rather with our idea of order; we have assigned exclusive meaning, importance and prominence to this one outcome and have bunched all the others together as having no order—or being *random*, as the technical term goes.

Seen from this arbitrary perspective, randomness appears to be the rule and order the improbable exception—and this in itself is a nice contradiction, warning us from the outset that stranger things may follow.

We usually think of a series of numbers as having no order, i.e., as being random, if it seems to us that no one digit or group of digits occurs much more frequently (or infrequently) than others. This is another way of saying that the series gives no clue that would enable us to predict what number will follow next. If, on the other hand, we examine the series 2, 5, 8, 11, we have little trouble predicting that the next number is most probably going to be 14, and that the rule underlying the series is incremental steps of three each.

Now assume that we are faced with the series 4, 1, 5, 9, 2, 6, 5, 3. As far as we can see, the series has no internal order, and assuming that further single digits are constantly being added to it by some sort of machine, we have no conceivable way of predicting the next digit more accurately than by one chance in ten. No sooner have we reached this conclusion than a mathematician shows us that the sequence is part of the number π (pi), namely its second to its tenth decimal digit. It thus turns out that this string of digits is anything but random; it is strictly and rigidly ordered, and any subsequent digit is fully predictable. In other words, our mistaken conclusion was based on our ignorance of its internal order.

All right, we say, but real random series must exist, and what we mean by "real" is that such series are free of any internal order, Spinoza notwithstanding. At this point, things become rather unbelievable to the layman, for there is now general agreement among most mathematicians that such a series does not and cannot exist. Their argument is intriguing:

Suppose we have a randomizing device° that prints out strings of single digits, and suppose further that somewhere in a very long and seemingly patternless string we come across the sequence 0123456789. Our first impression is that here the randomizer has broken down, for these ten digits are "obviously" fully patterned and therefore not random. But this is the same mistake we already made with the cards: the sequence 0123456789 is just as patterned or as random as any other combination of the ten digits.

The essence of randomness, writes G. Spencer Brown in his beautiful little book *Probability and Scientific Inference*,

> has been taken to be absence of pattern. But what has not hitherto been faced is that the absence of one pattern logically demands the presence of another. It is a mathematical contradiction to say that a series has no pattern; the most we can say is that it has no pattern that anyone is likely to look for. The concept of randomness bears meaning only in relation to the observer; if two observers habitually look for different kinds of pattern they are bound to disagree upon the series which they call random. [23]

With this we have re-entered, through a rear door, as it were, the field of communication—probably just at the moment the reader was beginning to wonder what all this had to do with the subject of this book. For once it is understood that contrary to general belief, order and chaos are not objective truths, but—like so many other things in life—determined by the perspective of the observer,† it

---

° The interested reader will find a brief description of such devices in Martin Gardner's article "On the Meaning of Randomness and Some Ways to Achieve It" [52].

† Of course, this principle had been formulated long before Brown, but it is still a bitter pill to swallow, for it threatens our belief in the

becomes possible to look at communication and certain disturbances of communication from a new vantage point. And we must be prepared for the possibility that our findings may differ sharply from accepted psychological, philosophical and even theological views.

But before turning to these, a brief excursion into another aspect of the phenomenon just described suggests itself because of its general relevance to our topic.

"Psychic" powers

Let us return once again to the business of constructing, as best we can, a series of random numbers, using, say, a ten-position spinner designed to randomize the ten digits of our decimal system. We have seen that as our string grows in length, certain regularities are bound to occur, which from a certain point on we can no longer ignore, since they threaten the random nature of our series. If, for instance, the number 2 were to occur noticeably more often than any other digit, we would have to start eliminating some of these 2s to bring their overall probability back down to approximately that of the other numbers. We have to do this, because otherwise the series would show a bias in favor of the occurrence of 2; it would not be random enough. We continue to *corriger la fortune* (as the French would call our method of additionally randomizing the randomization), construct a fairly long string of digits and hand it over to a

---

consistency and the order of the world. In a famous conversation with Einstein in 1926, even a genius like Heisenberg still maintained that only observable magnitudes should go into the making of a theory. Einstein, who had at one time himself postulated this, is supposed to have answered, "It is quite wrong to try founding a theory on observable magnitudes alone. *In reality the very opposite happens. It is the theory which decides what we can observe.*" (Italics mine.)

statistician for an examination of its randomness. We are surprised at his diagnosis, for he shows us that in this series of ours there is a strange, recurring pattern: certain regularities build up to values way above probability and suddenly drop again to insignificance. He is, of course, referring to our correcting the improbably improbable *as soon as we were aware of it.*

Precisely the same pattern can be found in many extrasensory perception experiments, notably in card guessing. As already mentioned, these experiments consist in having a subject guess the sequence of cards, each bearing one of five symbols. In this two-party interaction between experimenter and subject, some people's correct guesses reach levels high above statistical probability (this being, of course, one in five, since there are five symbols involved), and this is taken to show that the subject possesses extrasensory powers. The powers are, however, capriciously unreliable—they tend to disappear almost as quickly as they appear in the course of the experiment. To the best of my knowledge, it was G. Spencer Brown who first pointed out the similarity of random sequences and ESP experiments. We may be presented, he suggests,

with the spectacle of a particular kind of bias first building up to great significance, then gradually diminishing. This is indeed frequently observed in psychical research. But what is much more dramatic is the sort of significance which has built up over a period and which is suddenly noticed by the experimenter, after which it disappears completely. This sort of occurrence has become so common that ardent psychical researchers . . . have attempted to devise means of preventing it in the planning of their experiments. These means consist mainly of never looking to see if anything peculiar is happening until the end of the experiment. [24]

And in an appendix to his book he makes the intriguing claim that one can run ESP experiments with a table of random numbers instead of a human subject and arrive at results identical with those achieved by psychic researchers. Since his hypothesis is somewhat complicated, the reader is referred directly to the source [25], which provides starting points for potentially very interesting and novel research projects.

In any case, the fact that the entire meaning of a sequence can change as a result of the order imposed on it is an important aspect of communicational interaction and leads to our next subject.

6

Punctuation

There is a joke, known to most psychology students, in which a laboratory rat says of its experimenter, "I have trained that man so that every time I press this lever, he gives me food." Obviously the rat sees the S-R (stimulus-response) sequence quite differently than the experimenter does. To the experimenter, the rat's pressing the lever is a conditioned reaction to a preceding stimulus administered by him, while to the rat, the pressing of the lever is its stimulus administered to the experimenter. To the human, the food is a reward; to the rat, a reaction. In other words, the two *punctuate* the communicational sequence differently.°

° Since I have dealt with this phenomenon in greater detail elsewhere [176], I want to limit myself here to less theoretical examples. I shall

Ordering sequences in one way or another creates what, without undue exaggeration, may be called different realities. This is particularly evident in certain kinds of human conflict. A mother may see herself as the bridge between her husband and her children: if it were not for her, there would be no bond or contact between him and them. Far from sharing this view, the husband sees her as an obstacle between him and his children: if it were not for her constant interference and monitoring, he could have a much closer and more cordial relationship with them. If we do not bear in mind that this is a problem of punctuation—and not of one way of *behaving* rather than another—we may become victims of the same fallacy as the two parents and consider one of them mad or bad, the typical charges made when communication breaks down as a result of the discrepant punctuation of jointly experienced sequences of behavior. Just as with the rat and the experimenter, it is not the events themselves that they see differently, but their supposed order, and this gives them diametrically opposed meanings.

A husband believes that his wife dislikes to be seen with him in public. As "proof" he describes an occasion when they were late for an engagement, and as they were walking briskly from their car she kept staying behind him. "No

---

therefore side-step the question of why it is necessary to punctuate, i.e., impose an order, or *Gestalt*, on the sequences of events surrounding and involving any living being, and merely point to the obvious: without this order the world would appear truly random—that is, chaotic, unpredictable and extremely threatening. The Gestalt psychologists showed as early as the 1920s that this ordering is embedded in the deepest layers of our perceptions' neurophysiology, and its effect can be followed from there up to the highest levels of human functioning to, for example, creative activities and humor, as in the joke where a man arrives in heaven and finds an old friend sitting there with a luscious young woman on his lap. "Heaven indeed," says the newcomer, "is she your reward?" "No," replies the old man sadly, "I am her punishment." Clearly this is a matter of punctuation!

matter how much I slowed down," he explains, "she always stayed several steps behind me." "That is not true," she retorts indignantly. "No matter how fast I walked, he always kept several steps ahead of me."

In this case it was not the partners' individual punctuations that led to their two different views of the same occasion, but the other way around: they already had a discrepant view of their relationship and therefore tended to punctuate according to their individual views. This is very much in keeping with Einstein's remark: "It is the theory which decides what we can observe." But in human relationships the "theory" is itself the outcome of punctuation, and we run into a chicken-and-egg problem as to which came first—the problem or the punctuation. People remain consistently unaware of their discrepant views and naïvely assume that there is only *one* reality and *one* right view of it (namely their own); therefore anyone who sees things differently must be either mad or bad. But there is strong evidence that in the interaction between organisms there is a circular pattern: cause produces effect, and effect feeds back on cause, becoming itself a cause [177]. The result is very much like two people trying to communicate while speaking two different languages, or two players trying to play a game with two separate sets of rules.

During the last years of World War II and the early postwar years, hundreds of thousands of U.S. soldiers were stationed in or passed through Great Britain, providing a unique opportunity to study the effects of a large-scale penetration of one culture by another. One interesting aspect was a comparison of courtship patterns. Both American soldiers and British girls accused one another of being sexually brash. Investigation of this curious double charge brought to light an interesting punctuation problem. In both cultures, courtship behavior from the first eye contact to the ultimate consummation went through approximately thirty steps, but the sequence of these steps was different. Kissing, for instance, comes relatively early in the North American pattern (occupying, let us say, step 5) and relatively late in the English pattern (at step 25, let us assume), where it is considered highly erotic behavior. So when the U.S. soldier somehow felt that the time was right for a harmless kiss, not only did the girl feel cheated out of twenty steps of what for her would have been proper behavior on his part, she also felt she had to make a quick decision: break off the relationship and run, or get ready for intercourse. If she chose the latter, the soldier was confronted with behavior that according to *his* cultural rules could only be called shameless at this early stage of the relationship.

If we were to commit the mistake of looking at the girl's behavior in isolation, without taking into account its interactional nature, we would have no difficulty making a psychiatric diagnosis: if she suddenly runs, she is behaving hysterically; if she offers herself sexually, she is a nymphomaniac. Here again we are faced with a conflict that cannot and must not be reduced to the madness or badness of one partner, since it lies exclusively in the nature of their communication impasse.° It is in the nature of these disinformation problems that the partners cannot resolve them, for, as Wittgenstein once remarked, "What we cannot think, we cannot think; we cannot therefore say what we cannot think" [187]—or, as Ronald D. Laing put it: "If I don't know I know, I think I don't know" [83].

° This example could well have been included in Part I as another illustration of a "translation" mistake.

7

Semantic Punctuation

Punctuation also reaches into the field of semantics. Without clear indicators, it is at times impossible to decide where and how a string of words should be punctuated, and several different meanings may be conceivable. For instance, Professor Colin Cherry, an expert on telecommunications at the Imperial College in London, has pointed out that the sentence "Do you think that one will do?" [31] has a variety of meanings, depending upon which word is stressed. "Do you think *that* one will do?" "Do you think that *one* will do?" "Do *you* think that one will do?" all mean something quite different.

In written language we stress words by underlining them or printing them in italics, but these are much clumsier devices than the rich nuances of spoken language—tonal stress, pauses, gestures. Written language is therefore often more ambiguous, especially if the words are not embedded in a sufficiently self-explanatory context. "Growing pains" may refer either to pains that are becoming worse or to the pains connected with growing up. This kind of ambiguity occurs frequently in newspaper headlines, which must by nature be as short and informative as possible and are therefore often open to more than one interpretation. "Air Force Bars Sending Parcels to Vietnam" and "Topless Club Loses Appeal," to use two actual examples, both offer two quite separate meanings: that the Air Force had stopped sending parcels to Vietnam or that the Air Force had bars which were sending parcels to Vietnam; that topless night-club entertainment had lost its appeal to customers or (as was actually the case) that a particular night club had lost its legal appeal to continue employing topless waitresses. The legendary restaurant sign "Customers who think that our waiters are rude should see the manager" is also open to two very different interpretations.

All these mistakes could easily be made by a computer designed to translate from one language into another. According to an unconfirmed story, such a mechanical brain managed to misunderstand the seemingly unambiguous meaning of the sentence "Time flies like an arrow." Many people indeed find it difficult to imagine what the computer could possibly have thought was meant.°

Significantly, until communication research began to look into these patterns, the problems of this kind of disinformation were mostly the domain of literature. The tragic, fateful inescapability of these conflicts, in which no one is really to blame, yet everybody blames everybody else, the impossibility of reconciling incompatible views of reality seem to have intrigued writers since antiquity. A famous modern example

° Well, since *fruit flies* like a banana, how could the computer know that there are no such insects as *time flies* which happen to like an arrow?

is Akutagawa's story *In the Forest*, which the reader may know in its film version, *Rashomon*. It depicts the same sequence of events—the rape of a woman and the murder of her husband by a bandit, all witnessed by a woodcutter—seen through the eyes of these four persons. Akutagawa masterfully shows the emergence of as many separate "realities"—and not just the banal fact that the perception of witnesses is notoriously unreliable, as some of the reviewers emphasized—imperceptibly leading the reader to recognize the impossibility of deciding which of these realities is the "real" one. A detailed study of this phenomenon in literature, with all its philosophical implications regarding concepts of truth, destiny and transcendence, could make an interesting and unusual subject for a doctoral thesis.

Where everything is true, and so is its contrary

Hermann Hesse, in his little-known essay *In Sight of Chaos*, finds that this final dissolution of "reality" as we naïvely tend to think of it is particularly pronounced in Dostoevski's work. For Hesse, Prince Myshkin, the protagonist of *The Idiot*, "does not break the Tables of the Law, he simply turns them round and shows that the contrary to them is written on the other side" [70]. But it is in the story of the Grand Inquisitor in *The Brothers Karamazov* [36] that Dostoevski has given a supreme example of this phenomenon, perhaps equaled only by Kafka's two great novels, *The Trial* and *The Castle*.

Ivan Karamazov, an atheist, and his deeply religious younger brother, Alyosha, are engaged in a metaphysical argument. Ivan cannot reconcile himself to the existence of suffering, especially the suffering of young, innocent children. He has therefore come to the conclusion that even if all this suffering were a necessary precondition for final, perpetual harmony, he would not want that harmony: ". . . too high a price is asked for harmony; it's beyond our means to pay so much to enter on it. And so I hasten to give back my entrance ticket, and if I am an honest man I am bound to give it back as soon as possible. And that I am doing. It's not God that I don't accept, Alyosha, only I most respectfully return Him the ticket." Alyosha counters by bringing up the one being who has the right to forgive all of mankind's suffering—Christ. Ivan has expected this objection and in answer tells Alyosha his prose poem of the Grand Inquisitor.

The story is laid in sixteenth-century Seville, at the height of the Inquisition. On the day following a magnificent auto-da-fé, in which nearly one hundred heretics were burned alive, *ad majorem gloriam Dei*, Jesus descends once more and is immediately recognized and worshiped by his tortured, suffering people. But the cardinal, the Grand Inquisitor, has Him arrested and thrown in prison. Night falls; the door of the dungeon opens and in comes the old, ascetic cardinal, alone. For a few minutes there is silence; then the Grand Inquisitor delivers the most profound and terrible attack against Christianity that has ever been conceived:

Jesus has betrayed mankind, for He deliberately rejected the only way in which men might have been made happy. This unique, irretrievable moment occurred when " 'the wise and dread spirit, the spirit of self-destruction and non-existence,' " tempted Him in the wilderness by asking Him three questions, expressing " 'in three words, three human phrases,' the whole future history of the world and of humanity—dost Thou believe,' " the Grand Inquisitor asks, " 'that all the wisdom of the earth united could have invented anything in depth and force equal to the three questions that were actually put to Thee . . . ?' " First, the spirit tempted Jesus by asking Him to turn stones into bread. But He refused because He wanted mankind free, and what would obedience be worth if it were bought with bread? In doing this, He deprived man of his deepest craving—to find someone all of mankind can worship together, who will take away the awesome burden of freedom. When Jesus refused the second temptation—to throw Himself from the pinnacle of the temple, " 'for it is written: the angels shall hold Him up lest he fall' "—He rejected miracles. But man cannot bear to be without miracles; if he is deprived of them, he immediately creates new ones. Jesus craved faith given freely, not based on miracles. But is man capable of that? Man is weaker and baser by nature than Jesus thought. " 'By showing him so much respect, Thou didst . . . cease to feel for him . . .' "

And then the Grand Inquisitor comes to the last temptation, the third gift that He rejected: to rule the world, to unite all mankind " 'in one unanimous and harmonious ant-heap, for the craving for universal unity is the third and last anguish of men. . . . We are not working with Thee but with *him*. . . . We have taken the sword of Caesar, and in taking it, of course, have rejected Thee and followed *him*. Oh, ages are yet to come of the confusion of free thought, of their science and cannibalism. . . . [But] we have corrected Thy work and have founded it upon *miracle, mystery* and *authority*. And men rejoiced that they were again led like sheep, and that the terrible gift that had brought them such suffering, was, at last, lifted from their hearts. . . . And all will be happy, all the millions of creatures except the hundred thousand who rule over them. For only we, who guard the mystery, shall be unhappy. . . . Peacefully they will die, peacefully they will expire in Thy name, and beyond the grave they will find nothing but death.' " In concluding his terrible accusation, the Grand Inquisitor tells Jesus that He will not be allowed to bring unhappiness to mankind a second time—tomorrow He Himself will burn at the stake!

To all of this Jesus has listened in silence. Now He suddenly approaches the old man and softly kisses him on his thin, bloodless lips. The cardinal shudders, goes to the door and opens it: " 'Go, and come no more . . . come not at all, never, never!' " And the prisoner goes out into the night.

"But . . . that's absurd!" he [Alyosha] cried, flushing. "Your poem is in praise of Jesus, not in blame of Him—as you meant it to be . . ." [37].

Ever since the publication of *The Brothers Karamazov*, Alyosha's exclamation has been repeated over and over again. What does this story, written by a deeply religious man whose eyes filled with tears whenever Christ's name was mentioned irreverently in his presence, "really" mean; a story put into the mouth of a character whose atheism, Dostoevski tells us, is so profound that it represents the last step before complete faith; a story that anticipates what was to happen in the author's homeland forty years later?

The story is fictional, but its implications are very real. Christ and the Grand Inquisitor have both devoted their lives to the alleviation of suffering, and yet they are poles apart. Between them the paradox of help and of the power inevitably associated with help arises in all its stark contradiction. We have met it earlier, in the trivial story of the Albanian interpreter (page 13); now it hits us with its full metaphysical force. Jesus, the Grand Inquisitor charges, wants spontaneous compliance and thereby creates a paradox that is beyond human power to resolve. How can the weak be free? For the cardinal, the only solution is to rid man of the terrible burden of freedom; to make him unfree but happy. For Jesus, man's goal is not happiness but freedom. Ivan Karamazov's poem means something totally different if we accept only Christ's or only the Grand Inquisitor's world view. Those who grasp both views are left hanging in a universe where everything is true, and so is its contrary.

Somebody must have been telling lies about Joseph K., for without having done anything wrong he was arrested one morning. Thus begins Kafka's enigmatic novel *The Trial*. The trial never takes place; K. is neither free nor incarcerated; the Court never tells him the nature of the charges against him; he is supposed to know them, and his ignorance is further proof of his culpability. When he tries to get information from the Court, he is accused of impatience or impertinence; when he tries to ignore the Court's authority or simply wait for their next move, he is blamed for indifference or obduracy. In one of the final scenes, K. is talking to the prison chaplain in the cathedral, and the priest, after another of K.'s many attempts to gain some certainty about his fate, tries to "explain" K.'s situation by telling him the following parable:

Before the Law stands a doorkeeper on guard. To this doorkeeper there comes a man from the country who begs for admittance to the Law. But the doorkeeper says that he cannot admit the man at the moment. The man, on reflection, asks if he will be allowed, then, to enter later. "It is possible," answers the doorkeeper, "but not at this moment." Since the door leading into the Law stands open as usual and the doorkeeper steps to one side, the man bends down to peer through the entrance. When the doorkeeper sees that, he laughs and says: "If you are so strongly tempted, try to get in without my permission. But note that I am powerful. And I am only the lowest doorkeeper. From hall to hall, keepers stand at every door, one more powerful than the other. Even the third of these has an aspect that even I cannot bear to look at."

The man is given a stool and permitted to sit down at the side of the door, and there he sits for many years. Again and again he tries to get admission, or to get at least a definitive answer, but he is always told that he cannot enter yet. At long last his life is drawing to a close.

Before he dies, all that he has experienced during the whole time of his sojourn condenses in his mind into one question, which he has never yet put to the doorkeeper. He beckons the doorkeeper, since he can no longer raise his stiffening body. The doorkeeper has to bend far down to hear him, for the difference in size between them has increased very much to the man's disadvantage. "What do you want to know now?" asks the doorkeeper, "you are insatiable." "Everyone strives to attain the Law," answers the man, "how does it come about, then, that in all these years no one has come seeking admittance but me?" The doorkeeper perceives that the man is at the end of his strength and that his hearing is failing, so he bellows in his ear: "No one but you could gain admittance through this door, since this door was intended only for you. I am now going to shut it."

"So the doorkeeper deluded the man," says K. immediately. But the priest carefully and convincingly proves to him that the doorkeeper cannot be blamed, that he even went far beyond his duty to help the man. K. is perplexed but cannot dismiss the cogency of the priest's long interpretation. "You have studied the story more exactly and for a longer time than I," he concedes. "So you think that the man was not deluded?" "Don't misunderstand me," warns the priest and proceeds to show that there is another interpretation which proves that the deluded person is really the doorkeeper. And so convincing is this second exegesis that in the end K. is forced to agree again: "This is well argued, and I am inclined to agree that the doorkeeper is deluded." But again the priest immediately finds fault with K.'s agreement, for to doubt the doorkeeper's integrity is to doubt the Law itself. "I don't agree with that point of view," says K., shaking his head, "for if one accepts it, one must accept as true everything the doorkeeper says. But you yourself have sufficiently proved how impossible it is to do that." "No," says the priest, "it is not necessary to accept everything as true, one must only accept it as necessary." "A melancholy conclusion," says K. "It turns lying into a universal principle" [76].

And with this their dialogue ends on the same exhausted, ambiguous note that pervades all of K.'s attempts to reach an understanding. Every time he thinks he has succeeded in putting the bewildering sequences of events surrounding him in order, he is shown that it is not the "right" order. The priest's last words are: "The Court makes no claims upon you. It receives you when you come and it relinquishes you when you go." Kafka's K., like Dostoevski's Prince Myshkin, lives in a world where the Tables of the Law can be turned around and reveal that the contrary to them is written on the other side. Behind Myshkin the doors of an insane asylum close forever, and K. is eventually killed by two envoys of the Court.

The "Divine Experimenter"

K. never meets the Court; he meets only its messengers, agents and henchmen. Authority never reveals itself and never states its case against him, and yet K.'s entire life, every day and every act, is pervaded by its invisible presence. Exactly the same thing takes place in Kafka's other novel, *The Castle*, where K., the land surveyor, tries unsuccessfully to reach the authorities of the Castle who have hired him, but keep him down in the village and send him their enigmatic communications only through officials who are as low-ranking as the doorkeeper.

A purely fictional situation? Not at all. Most of us are embarked on an interminable quest for meaning and tend to assume the actions of a secret experimenter behind even the relatively trivial vicissitudes of our daily lives. Not too many of us can adopt the equanimity of the King of Hearts in

Alice in Wonderland, who manages to shrug off the nonsense poem by the White Rabbit with the philosophical remark: "If there is no meaning in it, that saves a world of trouble, you know, as we needn't try to find any."

A fairly large number of people, for example, have a private mythology about traffic lights. Reason may tell them that these lights are either rigidly set to turn from yellow to red to green with unchanging regularity or are controlled by sensor loops embedded in the street surface. But on another level they are convinced that the lights are working against them, predictably turning yellow and red just as they approach them. This may be considered a minipsychosis, but it is strong enough to cause real anger and make those who hold this idea feel that life or fate or nature or some sort of divine experimenter is against them. Consequently, any time a light does turn yellow or red, this chance event "registers" with them, while a green light passes virtually unnoticed. Once such an order (punctuation) has been read into the sequence of events, it becomes self-reinforcing. The same mechanism is at work in reality distortions of clinical magnitude: once the original premise has been formed and has taken hold, the rest of the delusion is patiently built up by seemingly logical deduction from this one absurd premise. Even more worrisome, these premises may be contagious. To hear somebody talk about his traffic-light problem can induce the same selective attention in the listener, to whom this odd idea never occurred before. This accounts for both rumors and mass psychoses, as two recent, rather remarkable events show.

The windshield mystery

In the late fifties the city of Seattle was plagued by a strange phenomenon: the windshields on more and more cars were found to be pockmarked by tiny indented scars. The situation grew so serious that at the governor's request, President Eisenhower sent a team of experts from the National Bureau of Standards to investigate the mystery. To quote Don D. Jackson, the founder and first director of the Mental Research Institute in Palo Alto:

> [They] quickly found two theories rampant to explain the cause of the pitting. The "fallout" theorists insisted that recent atomic tests by the Russians had contaminated the atmosphere, and this, aided by Seattle's moist climate, produced fallout that was returning to earth in a glass-etching dew. The "macadam" theorists maintained that Governor Rosollini's ambitious highway program was producing endless stretches of recently macadamized roads. These roads, again with the help of Seattle's foggy, foggy dew, were flinging acid drops against the heretofore unviolated windshields.
>
> Rather than investigate either theory, the Bureau of Standards men (bless them) turned their attention to a more primary issue. They established the fact that there was *no increase* in windshield pitting in Seattle at all. [75]

What had taken place was a kind of mass hysteria: as the reports on windshield pitting came to the attention of more and more people, they began to check their own cars. Most of them did this by looking closely at the glass from the outside, instead of looking through it, as usual, from inside the car. This revealed the pitting that is almost invariably caused by normal wear on a windshield. What had broken out in Seattle was an epidemic not of windshield pitting, but of windshield *viewing*.

Here again a perfectly natural, minor phenomenon (so minor in fact that nobody had bothered to pay attention to it before) was suddenly associated with emotionally laden issues (Soviet "fallout" and the ecologically questionable road-construction program), and by its own momentum reached self-confirming proportions that involved more and more people.

The Orléans rumor

The second example is more serious. It was later painstakingly reconstructed by a team of French sociologists headed by Edgar Morin, who wrote a book about it [109].

In May 1969, France was in the grip of the political instability created by De Gaulle's loss of a politically decisive (and, incidentally, actually insignificant) referendum and his final withdrawal from public life to Colombey-les-Deux-Églises. Elections were scheduled for June 1, and there was a general feeling of uncertainty. In the midst of this tense atmosphere, a sensational rumor began to spread in the city of Orléans. It began among the girl students of the local lycée and quickly spilled over to the general population. It alleged that the women's clothing shops and *boutiques* in this modern, provincial city of 100,000 were engaged in white-slave traffic; that female customers were overpowered and drugged in the fitting rooms,° held prisoner in cellars until night and then taken through subterranean passages to the banks of the Loire, where they were picked up by a submarine† and shipped overseas to suffer "a fate worse than death." By May 20, additional, very concrete information began to circulate: twenty-eight

---

° "The notion of the fitting room as a trap, as a clandestine antichamber to mystery and danger, turns up in the lower reaches of mass culture; the world of pulp fiction provides examples of it, and so does sensational journalism" [110].

† Morin reports that the president of the Jewish Committee of Orléans later swore that he had launched the submarine rumor as a joke and had it reported back to him twenty-four hours later as sober truth [111].

young women had already disappeared; one shoe store used spring-activated hypodermic needles concealed in the shoes, and so on.

The shopkeepers themselves were unaware of the rumor until the eve of the elections, May 31, when angry crowds began to gather in the streets outside their stores. But they had received strange telephone calls—one caller, for example, wanted to know the address of a brothel in Tangiers, another requested a delivery of "fresh meat."

As the rumor spread and became increasingly specific, two significant elements emerged: first, the shops in question were selling the new miniskirts and thus were associated in the provincial mind with a special sort of eroticism; second, the rumor was decidedly anti-Semitic, involving the age-old theme of ritual murder. By May 30 the leaders of the Jewish community were sufficiently alarmed to urge the authorities to intervene. The latter, of course, had already received information about the strange development, but had so far looked at the situation from a purely factual, public-safety point of view; they had found no concrete evidence whatsoever. Not a single female, let alone twenty-eight, had been reported missing in Orléans. But in limiting themselves to the facts, the authorities overlooked the most important one—that the problem was not the *truth* of the rumor, but its existence. They were faced with yet another of those typical human situations in which "validity depends on belief" [146]. The possibility of a pogrom was undeniable.

Meanwhile the outcome of the elections lessened the general tension, and soon the sane elements in the community began to take the upper hand; the rumor was pursued and shown to be unfounded. The press, private citizens and civic organizations united in a sharp rejection of anti-Semitism, and the story died even more quickly than it had arisen.

Clearly, this example goes a step beyond the preceding ones, in which the crucial premise had at least some semblance of reality. Traffic lights often do turn red as we approach them, and windshields do get pitted. But this last example shows that in constructing a specific "reality," the human mind can dispense with even that flimsy kind of evidence—a firm superstition is powerful enough, especially if it is shared by many others, as anti-Semitism is. And even if, as in the Orléans case, the rumor turns out to be absurd, there is always a maxim that allows the believer to save face.* "Where there's smoke, there's fire" is one such saying ("but a pile of fresh manure will do just as well," the writer Roda Roda used to add).

A particularly glaring example of this tendency deserves to be mentioned briefly. A stock in trade of anti-Semitism is the infamous *Protocols of the Elders of Zion*, in which the anonymous author lays out the grand strategy for Jewish world domination, leaving no doubt that this is the ultimate aim of international Jewry. In its issues of August 16, 17 and 18, 1921, the London *Times* carried a series of articles about the origins of this work, revealing that its source was a book by the French lawyer Maurice Joly, published in 1864 in Brussels under the title *Dialogue aux enfers entre Montesquieu et Machiavel*. As Joly later explained in his autobiography, the *Dialogue* was an attempt to attack the despotic rule of Napoleon III under the guise of a conversation in hell between Montesquieu and Machiavelli, with the former presenting the case for liberalism but being quickly defeated by the brilliance of Machiavelli's cynical defense of despotism. By seemingly extolling what he wanted to attack, Joly hoped that the reader of the *Dialogue* would get the

---

* In fact, some young Orléanais told members of the Morin team: "When a whole town says the same thing, there has to be something in it" [113].

point. He was only too right in this assumption; the French secret police immediately got the point. They confiscated the copies of the book that had been smuggled into France and arrested the author. He was tried and sentenced to fifteen months' imprisonment.

So far, the matter had no relation whatsoever to the Jews. The book might indeed have served as a source of inspiration to a young Hitler. It recommends that a modern ruler should merely pretend to observe the outward signs of legality, should have a subservient popular assembly rubber-stamp and legalize his decisions, a secret police to deal with any opposition, and should generally override his subjects' pangs of conscience by dazzling military victories over external foes.

The unknown forger of the *Protocols* simply appropriated all of this and made it appear to be the long-range program of a powerful secret body, the Elders of Zion. To quote from historian Norman Cohn:

> In all, over 160 passages in the *Protocols*, totalling two-fifths of the entire text, are clearly based on passages in Joly; in nine of the chapters the borrowings amount to more than half of the text, in some they amount to three-quarters, in one (Protocol VII) to almost the entire text. Moreover, with less than a dozen exceptions, the order of the borrowed passages remains the same as it was in Joly, as though the adaptor had worked through the *Dialogue* mechanically, page by page, copying straight into his "protocols" as he proceeded. Even the arrangement in chapters is much the same—the twenty-four chapters of the *Protocols* correspond-ing roughly with the twenty-five of the *Dialogue*. Only towards the end, where the prophecy of the Messianic Age predominates, does the adaptor allow himself any real independence of his model. [34]

Ever since, the *Protocols* have played an important role in anti-Semitism, and no matter what attempts have been made to reveal their fraudulent nature, these very attempts are seen as further proof that there must be some truth in them. Otherwise why would the Elders try so hard to prove their falseness? This is a classical example of a self-sealing premise, i.e., a premise that is vindicated by proof as well as disproof. It is also identical with the way the paranoid punctuates his interaction with others: he "knows" they are out to hurt him, and if they try to assure him of their friendly intentions, or especially if they point out to him that his suspicions are unfounded, this "proves" that they are out to get him—for why would they otherwise try so hard to convince him?

Something very similar happened at the height of the Orléans rumor when the police declared that there was no substance to the whole thing, that not a single female had been reported missing. This merely "proved" that the police were themselves involved. "It was alleged," the chief of the Criminal Investigation Department told a reporter of the *Aurore*, "that I had made ten million francs that way. I suppose the more exaggerated and extravagant a story is, the more people are likely to believe it" [114].

We are now in a position to appreciate more clearly how the two conclusions that can be drawn from the Bavelas experiment (pages 48–51) apply to real-life situations. There, as in the cases we have just examined, events contradicting the "explanation" lead not to its correction, but rather to its further elaboration, and the more abstruse and objectively unbelievable the pseudoexplanation is, the more readily it is believed.

There is something compelling and fateful about the initial premise in a context of disinformation, from which everything else follows almost necessarily. But the idea that this is how "realities" are created is difficult for most of us to accept. We are far more willing to imagine the workings of some secret power behind the way things turn out, or—if we are more psychology-minded—some law of the mind. But as Schopenhauer pointed out, the study of the assumed purposes and designs in nature

> is brought into nature only by the intellect, which thus marvels at a miracle that it has created itself in the first place. It is (if I may explain so sublime a matter with a trivial simile) the same as if the intellect were astonished at finding that all multiples of nine again yield nine when their single figures are added together, or else to a number whose single figures again add up to nine; and yet it has itself prepared this miracle in the decimal system. [160]

It seems that we shall have to reconcile ourselves to a far less "sophisticated" idea of the origin of world views than metaphysics and psychology have taught us—one that is based simply on the interaction between two elementary ingredients: chance and necessity, precisely the matrix that has been proposed by some biologists, notably by Nobel Prize-winner Jacques Monod, as the origin of life:

> The initial elementary events which open the way to evolution in the intensely conservative systems called living beings are microscopic, fortuitous, and utterly without relation to whatever may be their effects upon teleonomic functioning.
> But once incorporated in the DNA structure, the accident—*essentially unpredictable because always singular*—will be mechanically and faithfully replicated and translated: that is to say, both multiplied and transposed into millions or billions of copies. *Drawn out of the realm of pure chance, the accident enters into that of necessity, of the most implacable certainties.* For natural selection operates at the macroscopic level, the level of organisms.
> Even today a good many distinguished minds seem unable

to accept or even to understand that from a source of noise natural selection alone and unaided could have drawn all the music of the biosphere. In effect natural selection operates *upon* the products of chance and can feed nowhere else; but it operates in a domain of very demanding conditions, and from this domain chance is barred. It is not to chance but to these conditions that evolution owes its generally progressive course, its successive conquests, and the impression it gives of a smooth and steady unfolding. [103] (Italics mine.)

9

Experimental Disinformation

Experimentally produced states of disinformation shed a great deal of light on how these situations affect people in real life. In one such experiment, attempted years ago at the Mental Research Institute in Palo Alto, we asked Dr. Don D. Jackson, internationally known as an expert on the psychotherapy of schizophrenia, if he was willing to let himself be filmed in an initial interview with a paranoid patient who thought he was a clinical psychologist. Dr. Jackson agreed. We then asked a clinical psychologist who was also doing psychotherapy with psychotics if he was willing to let himself be filmed in an initial interview with a paranoid patient who thought he was a psychiatrist. He, too, agreed. So we brought the two doctors together in a sort of super-therapy session in which both promptly went to work, treating each other for his "delusions." For our purposes, the situation could hardly have been more perfect: thanks to their peculiar state of disinformation, both behaved very appropriately and therapeutically, but the more sanely each of them acted, the crazier he appeared to the other. Unfortunately, the experiment broke down after a few minutes when the psychologist remembered that there was indeed a psychiatrist by the name of Dr. Jackson and immediately used the welcome opportunity to discuss his own problems gratis with a real expert for the rest of the interview.

Much more successful than this piece of research were the famous experiments by Professor Solomon Asch of the University of Pennsylvania, in which groups of seven to nine college students were shown two cards. On the first was a

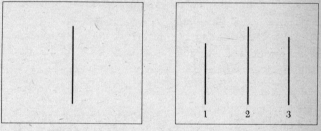

Card 1   Card 2

single vertical line, on the second three vertical lines of various lengths. The students were told that this was an experiment in visual perception and that their task was to identify the line on card 2 which was of the same length as the line on card 1. As Asch described the course of events:

> The experiment opens uneventfully. The subjects announce their answers in the order in which they have been seated in the room, and on the first round every person chooses the same matching line. Then a second set of cards is exposed; again the group is unanimous. The members appear

ready to endure politely another boring experiment. On the third trial there is an unexpected disturbance. One person near the end of the group disagrees with all the others in his selection of the matching line. He looks surprised, indeed incredulous, about the disagreement. On the following trial he disagrees again, while the others remain unanimous in their choice. The dissenter becomes more and more worried and hesitant as the disagreement continues in succeeding trials; he may pause before announcing his answer and speak in a low voice, or he may smile in an embarrassed way. [9]

What the dissenter does not know, Asch explains, is that the other students have been carefully briefed beforehand to give unanimously wrong answers at certain points. The dissenter is the only real subject of the experiment and finds himself in a most unusual and disquieting situation: he must either contradict the matter-of-fact opinion of the group and appear to be strangely confused or doubt the evidence of his senses. Unbelievable as it may seem, under these circumstances 36.8 percent of the subjects chose the second alternative and submitted to the misleading group opinion [11].

Asch then introduced certain modifications into the experiment and was able to show that the size of the opposition—that is, the number of people who contradicted the subject's answers—was of crucial importance. If only one member of the group contradicted him, the subject had little difficulty maintaining his independence. As soon as the opposition was increased to two persons, the subject's submission jumped 13.6 percent. With three opponents, the failure curve went up to 31.8 percent, whereupon it flattened out, and any further increase in the number of opponents raised the percentage only to the abovementioned 36.8 percent.

Conversely, the presence of a supporting partner was a

powerful help in opposing the group pressure; under these conditions the incorrect responses of the subject dropped to one fourth of the error rate mentioned above.

It is notoriously difficult to appreciate the impact of an event like an earthquake before having actually experienced one. The effect of the Asch experiment is comparable. When the subjects were let in on the scheme, they reported that during the test they had experienced varying degrees of emotional discomfort, from moderate anxiety to something akin to depersonalization. Even those who refused to submit to group opinion and continued to trust their own perceptions usually did so with nagging worries that they might, after all, be wrong. A typical statement was: "To me it seems I'm right, but my reason tells me I'm wrong, because I doubt that so many people could be wrong and I alone right."

Others resorted to very typical ways of rationalizing or explaining away the state of disinformation that undermined their world view: they either transferred the fear to an organic defect ("I began to doubt that my vision was right"), or they decided there was some exceptional complication (e.g., an optical illusion), or they became so suspicious that they refused to believe the final explanation, maintaining that it was itself part of the experiment and therefore not to be trusted. One of the subjects summed up what most of the successful dissenters apparently felt: "This is unlike any experience I have had in my life—I'll never forget it as long as I live" [10].

As Asch has pointed out, perhaps the most frightening factor in the subjects' blind surrender is the deep-seated longing to be in agreement with the group—almost in the way the Grand Inquisitor expressed this craving. The willingness to surrender one's independence, to barter the evidence of one's senses for the comfortable but reality-distorting satisfaction of feeling in harmony with a group is, of course, the stuff on which demagogues and dictators thrive.

There are two more conclusions, which, so far as I know, Asch has not drawn. The first is that the disinformation created by the experiment is virtually identical with that of a so-called schizophrenic and his family, except for the obvious fact that it is even more difficult to be a minority of one among one's closest relatives than it is in a group of one's peers. Almost invariably there is a myth in these families that they have no problems and none of their members is unhappy about anything, except that they have a mental patient in their midst. But even a brief interview with them reveals glaring inconsistencies and reality distortions within the family as a whole. Very much like the subject in the Asch experiment, the schizophrenic patient, who is usually the most perceptive member of the family, lives in a world that is constantly defined for him as normal. It would be an almost superhuman task to resist this pressure, to become a dissenter and expose the family myth. In all likelihood, such an action would simply be considered further evidence of madness. If the patient *were* capable of relying on the evidence of his senses, it would be at the price of risking rejection by his family (this time because of badness, not madness)—and especially if he is young, his family is the only place that seems safe to him. Like the subject in the Asch experiment, he is faced with the dilemma of either risking rejection or sacrificing the evidence of his senses—and he is much more likely than the experimental subject to choose the second alternative and remain a "patient."

The other point is this: if, as I have already mentioned in connection with intercultural problems (pages 7 and 63), one were to disregard the *interpersonal* communication context in which the Asch experiment took place and focused attention exclusively on the behavior of the subject, it would be easy to give a psychiatric diagnosis to his nervousness, his "inappropriate" anxiety and the glaring "reality distortions" of which he is a victim. This is by no means a hypothetical point; rather, the failure to take into account the interactional context in which a so-called psychiatric condition manifests itself is at the root of many a psychiatric diagnosis based on the medical model of illness as the manifestation of a sick organ (the brain or the mind). In this monadic perspective, madness or badness becomes the attribute of one individual who is obviously in need of therapy, and therapy becomes a reality distortion in its own right.*

Herr Slossenn Boschen's song

Long before Asch, the British humorist Jerome K. Jerome thought up a similar social entanglement in which not only the subject but also the group are victims of deliberately engineered disinformation. The story appears in his book *Three Men in a Boat (to say nothing of the dog)*. At a supper party two students inveigle a German guest, Professor Slossenn Boschen, into singing a German song. Before his arrival they explain to the other guests that there is something very special about it:

They said it was so funny that, when Herr Slossenn Boschen had sung it once before the German Emperor, he (the German Emperor) had had to be carried off to bed.
They said nobody could sing it like Herr Slossenn Boschen; he was so intensely serious all through it that you might fancy he was reciting a tragedy, and that, of course, made it all the funnier. They said he never once suggested by

* The literature on this subject is by now overwhelmingly large. As an introduction, the interested reader is referred to references 13, 40, 80, 84, 174.

his tone or manner that he was singing anything funny—that would spoil it.

Herr Boschen comes, sits down behind the piano to accompany himself, and the two young men take up unobtrusive positions behind his back. The narrator explains how things go from there:

I don't understand German myself. . . . Still, I did not want the people there to guess my ignorance; so I hit upon what I thought to be rather a good idea. I kept my eye on the two young students and followed them. When they tittered, I tittered; when they roared, I roared; and I also threw in a little snigger all by myself now and then, as if I had seen a bit of humor that had escaped the others. I considered this particularly artful on my part.

I noticed, as the song progressed, that a good many other people seemed to have their eye fixed on the two young men, as well as myself. These other people also tittered when the young men tittered, and roared when the young men roared; and, as the two young men tittered and roared and exploded with laughter pretty continuously all through the song, it went exceedingly well.

The professor first feigns surprise at the laughter, then he begins to scowl more and more fiercely. He finishes amid a shriek of laughter and leaps up.

He swore at us in German (which I should judge to be a singularly effective language for that purpose), and he danced, and shook his fists, and called us all the English he knew. He said he had never been so insulted in all his life.

It appeared that the song was not a comic song at all. It was about a young girl who lived in the Hartz Mountains, and who had given up her life to save her lover's soul; and he died, and met her spirit in the air; and then, in the last verse, he jilted her spirit, and went on with another spirit—I'm not quite sure of the details, but it was something very sad, I know. Herr Boschen said he had sung it once before the German Emperor, and he (the German Emperor) had sobbed like a little child. He (Herr Boschen) said it was generally acknowledged to be one of the most tragic and pathetic songs in the German language.

The guests look around for the two students, but they seem to have left quietly at the end of the song.

Candid Camera

Similar patterns are the stuff Allen Funt's television series, *Candid Camera*, and his films are made of. They are all based on specially contrived, unusual social situations or mind-boggling events, which are filmed without the subject's awareness, so that his reactions are quite genuine. In Funt's film, *What Do You Say to a Naked Lady?*, there is a very funny scene in which an elevator door opens and out steps a young lady, wearing only shoes, a hat, a strategically placed handbag and a smile. As if it were the most natural thing in the world, she turns to a man who happens to be waiting there and asks him where a certain office is. The same scene is filmed several times with different people and the camera records hilarious reactions: after getting over their surprise, some people behave as if this were Hans Christian Andersen's story of the Emperor's New Clothes and politely answer her question as if nothing were amiss; one man gets extremely worried and tries to wrap his raincoat around her. Only one dares to refer to the reality of the situation by stating wryly, "Pretty outfit you've got there."

Even here the line between good fun and terror is extremely fine, especially if Funt's humane restraint and sense of humor were lacking. In a European television series attempting to imitate *Candid Camera*, an unsuspecting driver is filmed as she enters a public garage and correctly parks her car in a space flanked by two pillars. As soon as she is gone, the crew arrives with a fork-lift truck, picks up her car, turns it around 90 degrees and places it straight between the two pillars with only a few inches left between them and the front and rear bumpers. The woman returns

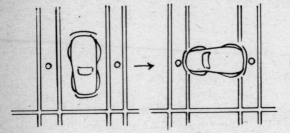

and cannot believe her eyes—not only can she not drive away, but the unimaginable impossibility of the situation visibly frightens her. She runs for help, and by the time she returns with the incredulous attendant, the crew has returned the car to its original position, so that in addition to her first shock, she now must doubt her sanity.

10
The Emergence of Rules

The stark terror that may be inherent in even relatively minor contexts of disinformation underlines the necessity to impose an order on events, to punctuate their sequence—a necessity shared by both humans and animals. If people find themselves in a situation so totally novel for them that past experience does not supply them with a precedent, they nonetheless punctuate it immediately, often without realizing it.

A simple example: a boy has his first date with a girl and she arrives twenty minutes late. Let us disregard the (very likely) possibility that he already has in his mind a rule regarding punctuality—e.g., that people should be punctual, or that women are never on time, or any other such premise. Let us instead assume that the novelty of this experience, coupled with the belief that girls are superhuman, angelic beings, makes him see a law of the universe in everything she does, so that he will not mention those twenty minutes by word or mien. By not commenting on her tardiness, he has let the first rule of their relationship be established:° she now has the "right" to be late, and he has "no right" to complain about it. In fact, if on a later occasion he were to criticize her for always making him wait, she would be justified in asking, "How come you are suddenly complaining about it?"

What this trivial example shows is that it is as impossible not to punctuate an interaction as it is to construct a random series. Rules are bound to emerge, and especially in human interaction, any interchange invariably reduces the possibilities which until that moment were open to the partners.† Another example is the emergence of rules in a newly formed psychotherapy group. There, too, certain behaviors become rules merely as a result of their occurrence and uncontested acceptance (or uncontested modification) by the other group members. In communications research, this phenomenon is called limitation and refers to the fact that every exchange of messages, however given, inevitably narrows the number of possible next moves [178]. In other words, even though a given event may never be officially mentioned, let alone officially approved, the mere fact that it happened and was tacitly accepted sets a precedent and thereby creates a rule. The breaking of such a rule then becomes intolerable, or at least wrong behavior. This is just as true for animals defining their territory as for interpersonal or international relations.

Spies are a case in point. Their existence and activities are

---

° Of course, a rule would also have been established if he had mentioned her delay.

† This points to the absurdity of modern "free marriage" arrangements, in which both spouses are supposedly free "to do their own thing."

neither officially admitted by their own country nor officially sanctioned by their host country. But over a period of time a pattern emerges: both countries silently tolerate the presence of a specific number of "official" spies, usually referred to as military, economic, cultural or press attachés. And faithful to the principle "If you kick my spy, I'll kick your spy," any action taken by one country against one of these official spies is immediately reciprocated by the other country. In addition to these official spies, there is usually a large number of "unofficial" ones not covered by this tacit agreement who, when caught, can be kicked from pillar to post with impunity.

The superpowers' mutual electronic surveillance is another example. The more closely these specially equipped ships and planes can approach the territory of the other nation, the better the results of their surveillance will be. But how close is too close—especially in a world in which territorial limits are still a matter of international dispute? The unwritten but officially unacknowledged rule appears to be: If a surveillance plane is shot down on its first approach to a particular area, the incident is kept quiet, but if it is shot down during the second flight on exactly the same route, this constitutes a serious international incident. Harvard economist and game-theory expert Thomas Schelling has described this interactional phenomenon:

> We seem to have some understanding about traffic rules for patrolling bombers; there are apparently certain lines we stay on this side of, lines the Russians presumably can recognize, the crossing of which they can probably monitor to some extent. This is certainly a restraint that we unilaterally observe in the interest of reducing misunderstanding and alarms. As far as I know, the traffic rules are communicated, not explicitly, but simply by behaving in accordance with them (perhaps *conspicuously* in accordance

with them) and possibly by having chosen the dividing lines in such a way that their significance is recognizable . . . *It seems doubtful whether this tacit understanding could be made much stronger by a written document.* [158] (Italics mine.)

In areas where spheres of influence between countries are not sufficiently defined and acknowledged, the situation is dangerously unstable and explosive, as Southeast Asia and the Middle East demonstrate. In such areas the contestants usually resort to what Hitler called salami tactic; that is, the technique of creating one accomplished fact after another, carefully keeping them sufficiently small so that no single fact is quite important enough for the other side to risk an all-out conflict over it.

11

Interdependence

> You tell me you are going to Fez.
> Now, if you say you are going to Fez,
> This means you are not going.
> But I happen to know you are going to Fez.
> Why are you lying to me who are my friend?
>
> Moroccan proverb

We all know what it means when one thing depends on another. But when the other thing depends on the first to an equal degree, so that they unavoidably influence each other, they are said to be interdependent. This is the case with the examples in the preceding chapter: the behavior of each party involved determines and is determined by that of the other. And we have already seen that this shift in perspective—the fact that most interaction is circular, with cause producing effect and effect turning into cause and feeding back to the original cause—leads to very different world views.

The Prisoner's Dilemma

The concept of interdependence is perhaps best introduced by the game-theoretical model of the Prisoner's Dilemma, formulated and named by Albert W. Tucker, a professor of mathematics at Princeton. In its original version, a district attorney is holding two men suspected of armed robbery. There is not enough evidence to take the case to court, so he has the two men brought to his office. He tells them that in order to have them convicted he needs a confession; without one he can charge them only with illegal possession of firearms, which carries a penalty of six months in jail. If they both confess, he promises them the minimum sentence for armed robbery, which is two years. If, however, only one confesses, he will be considered a state witness and go free, while the other will get twenty years, the maximum sentence. Then, without giving them a chance to arrive at a joint decision, he has them locked up in separate cells from which they cannot communicate with each other.

Under these unusual circumstances, what should they do? The answer seems simple: since half a year in prison is by far the lesser evil, it makes sense for them not to confess. But no sooner have they reached this conclusion in the solitude of their separate cells than a doubt arises in their minds: "What if my companion, who is bound to conclude correctly that this is what I am thinking, takes advantage of the situation and confesses? Then he goes scot-free and I get twenty years. On second thought, I am safer if I confess. Then, if he does not confess, I am the one who goes free." But immediately a new realization presents itself: "If I do this, I not only betray his trust in me to make the decision most advantageous for *both* of us (i.e., not to confess and get away with six months), but if he is as untrustworthy as this would make me, he will arrive at exactly the same conclusion. We will both confess and be sentenced to two years—a far worse outcome than the six months we could get if we both denied the crime."

This is their dilemma, and it has no solution. Even if the prisoners somehow succeeded in communicating with each other and reach a joint decision, their fate will still depend on whether each feels he can trust the other to stick to the decision—if not, the vicious circle will start all over again. And on further thought each will invariably realize that the trustworthiness of the other depends largely on how trustworthy he appears *to* the other, which in turn is determined by the degree of trust each of them has *for* the other—and so forth ad infinitum.

There is a vast literature about this particular pattern of interaction, the most authoritative work probably still being Anatol Rapoport and Albert M. Chammah's book [139]. An excellent, very concise summary of the nature of the Prisoner's Dilemma, its relation to such extrarational notions as trust and solidarity, and its place in modern mathematical thought can be found in a recent article by Rapoport in *Scientific American* [140].

The Prisoner's Dilemma is usually presented in the form of a four-cell matrix, based on the assumption that there are only two players, A and B, who both have two choices each, namely a_1 and a_2 for player A, and b_1 and b_2 for B. The figure on page 100 is such a matrix and shows simply that if A chooses a_1 and B chooses b_1, they will win five points each. If B chooses alternative b_2 instead, A will lose five points and B will win eight. The opposite happens if the outcome of their choice is a_2, b_1. Finally, if the outcome is a_2, b_2, they lose three points each. These payoffs are known to both players. Since the rules of the game are that the choices must be made simultaneously and without the

Player B:

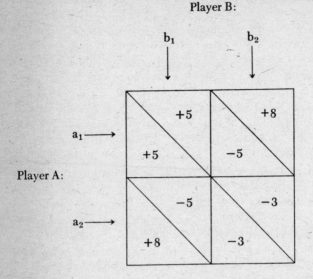

Player A:

possibility of communicating with the other player in order to reach an agreement (which the other player could, of course, break at any round of the game), this simple mathematical model contains in itself the essence and the hopelessness of the Prisoner's Dilemma, as the reader can easily convince himself by playing it with another person— preferably not a friend.

Actual situations of the Prisoner's Dilemma type are far more frequent than one might expect. They arise whenever two or more people are in a state of disinformation as a result of having to reach a joint decision about which, for one reason or another, they cannot communicate.

In human relations, especially marriages, communication is usually quite possible, yet the partners may be living in a chronic Prisoner's Dilemma situation if they do not trust each other enough to choose the alternatives most advantageous to *both* of them. In terms of the Prisoner's Dilemma matrix, they realize that the most reasonable and jointly desirable decision would be a_1, b_1, which offers both of them a comfortable gain. But as we have seen, this decision can be reached only through mutual trust; in the absence of such trust the only "safe" decision is a_2, b_2, which amounts to a joint life of quiet desperation.

Exactly the same dilemma has plagued disarmament talks, from the days of the League of Nations to the present. As one follows the course of these negotiations it becomes obvious that all nations agree on the goal: large-scale if not total disarmament. This goal can be reached only under conditions of mutual trust. But trust cannot be enforced or deliberately produced; indeed, it cannot even be defined as part of a treaty the way one can define the number of nuclear submarines or the details of an antiballistic weapons system. Thus a large part of these interminable negotiations seems to be wasted in an attempt to translate trust into a language that does not have a word for it. In the meantime, mankind is threatened with nuclear extinction, and the only sane alternative (decision a_1, b_1) is impossible. The negotiations go on and on in a vicious circle involving the other three cells of the matrix.

Is there any hope that nations will ever show that limited degree of trust which, at least occasionally, is displayed by individuals in comparable situations and enables them to escape the ultimately lethal trap of pure rationality? Nobody knows—but there is a ray of hope: in the course of the Nixon-Brezhnev talks in June 1974, the U.S. government made it clear that it had no intention of building the second antiballistic missile (ABM) ring to which it was entitled by the terms of the 1972 missile treaty. In the face of this unilateral decision, the Soviets seem to have felt it safe to forgo construction of their second ABM ring (behind the Ural Mountains)—a development which, with justification, was greeted as a historic breakthrough in relations between the two nations. This breakthrough became possible only after one side had unilaterally abandoned the language of pure rationality and taken a step in the belief that the other party would not take advantage of it. In other words, the United States exposed itself to all the risks that trust entails and which make it so "unreasonable."

This brings us to a final word on the Prisoner's Dilemma. When we said earlier that the paradox had no solution, we were right only within the framework of the situation existing between the district attorney and his two prisoners, i.e., the four-cell matrix. A fascinating addendum to this paradox has been presented by University of Pennsylvania mathematician Nigel Howard [74], involving what he calls a theory of metagames and proving that there is a solution at a higher level. A presentation of Howard's proof would go beyond the scope of this book; its importance, however, can hardly be overrated. As Rapoport summarizes the practical implications of Howard's resolution:

> In order to be intuitively understood and accepted, the formal solution of the Prisoner's Dilemma paradox still needs to be translated in a social context. When and if that is accomplished, Prisoner's Dilemma will deserve a place in the museum of famous ex-paradoxes where those of the incommensurables, Achilles and the tortoise and the barbers trying to decide if they ought to shave themselves, are enshrined. [140]

I leave it to the specialists in game theory to decide whether the breakthrough in the ABM treaty is not perhaps a first translation of Howard's solution in a social context.

What I think that he thinks that I think . . .

Aside from trust, the important factor in the Prisoner's Dilemma situation is the physical impossibility of communicating and thereby agreeing on the best decision. If an interdependent decision *must* be reached under these circumstances, what can be done? The answer is not simple, and as so often happens with sticky problems, the better question is: What must *not* be done?

Obviously, the decision must not be attempted on the basis of one's *own* best judgment (which is all that matters in a noninterdependent decision). Rather, my decision must be based on the best possible assumption about what the other will consider the best decision. And exactly as in the case of the two prisoners, his decision will in turn be determined by what *he* thinks that *I* think is the best decision. In absence of open and free communication, all interdependent decisions are based on this theoretically infinite regress of what I think that he thinks that I think that . . . Thomas Schelling, who in his book *The Strategy of Conflict* has dealt extensively with this pattern, uses the following situation as an example:

When a man loses his wife in a department store without any prior understanding on where to meet if they get separated, the chances are good that they will find each other. It is likely that each will think of some obvious place to meet, so obvious that each will be sure that the other is sure that it is "obvious" to both of them. One does not simply predict where the other will go, since the other will go where he predicts the first to go, which is wherever the first predicts the second to predict the first to go, and so on ad infinitum. Not "What would I do if I were she?" but

"What would I do if I were she wondering what she would do if she were I wondering what I would do if I were she . . . ?" [155]

In order to be successful, an interdependent decision made without direct communication must be based on some "world view" commonly held by the parties involved, on some tacitly shared assumption, or on some element that through its obviousness, its physical or metaphorical prominence or some other unique quality stands out far enough from the numerous other possibilities equally present in most situations. Schelling suggests that whimsy may send the man and his wife to the "Lost and Found" office, but we can imagine that if one of them did not share the other's sense of humor, they would never find each other that way.

To take another example, suppose two secret agents on a very important mission must meet, and that for some reason they know the place but not the time of their meeting. Since it is much too dangerous for them to hang around the place for the next twenty-four hours, how are they going to meet? What, they will both have to ask themselves, is the particular hour that the other will consider that I consider that he considers the most obvious? In this case the answer is relatively simple. There are only two points in the course of a twenty-four-hour day that clearly "stick out" above all other times: 12 noon and 12 midnight. It would clearly be foolish to expect the other to turn up at any hour which to *oneself* (for whatever personal reasons) might seem the most obvious or practical—unless, of course, he somehow knew about one's preference. Or suppose that the place of the secret meeting has not been pre-established either. The agents' task is greatly complicated, but not necessarily impossible. Even a large city, let alone a town or a rural area, has topographical points that literally "stick out" and thus offer themselves as the most obvious meeting places: an important bridge, the tallest building, the central square. Again, both agents will have to resist the naïve temptation simply to wait at a place that for personal, idiosyncratic reasons seems to be the best choice.

It is not easy to determine prominence in interdependent decisions, as Schelling has demonstrated by a simple experiment [156]. A group of people is shown the numbers 7, 100, 13, 99, 261, 555 and told that if they all choose the same number without discussing their choice among themselves, they will all win a large amount of money.

Which of these six numbers is prominent and thus the right choice for a joint decision? It should be (but usually is not) at once obvious to all the participants that their *personal* associations cannot possibly be used for their interdependent decision. For some people, 7 and 13 have great superstitious importance, but even among them there is difference of opinion about which is lucky or unlucky. The number 100 seems to offer itself to the more rational-minded as the square of 10, but others may consider 555 more pleasing and symmetrical.

Well, which is it? Most of the readers will probably strongly disagree, but actually, there is one and only one number that in the context of the other five is undeniably prominent, albeit *negatively* prominent: 261. It is the only one of the six with no superstition, popular belief or rationalization attached to it, the only "meaningless" number (unless it is part of, say, your address or telephone number, which would hardly confer universal prominence on it), and this *lack* of any particular meaning gives it prominence. If the reader can agree with this reasoning, he will see that interdependent decisions are tricky and require a good deal of thinking about thinking.

12

*We should therefore claim, in
the name of tolerance, the right
not to tolerate the intolerant.*

—Karl Popper, *The Open Society
and Its Enemies*

Let us consider the following matrix:

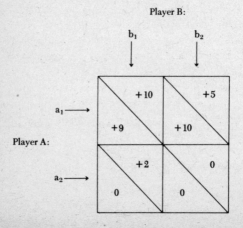

If, as in our previous game, the players move simultaneously and without prior communication, B wins easily by choosing b_1, since, assuming that A is a rational player, A is bound to choose a_1 (a_2 would give him 0). If, however, we now assume that the players can communicate with each other and make their moves successively, the situation changes completely. A can announce that he will choose a_2 unless B chooses b_2, so that if he (A) is successful, the outcome will be a_1, b_2—which gives A the better payoff (10), while B fares only half as well. Quite naturally, A will have to communicate something in addition to his mere announcement, namely a plausible reason to convince B that he (A) would indeed resort to his somewhat suicidal choice of a_2 unless B complies.

What we have here is the essence of the interpersonal, interdependent phenomenon of a *threat*, a demand for certain behavior, coupled with the announcement of specific consequences that will follow if the other party does not comply. There are, of course, other, more comprehensive definitions of threat—the reader is again referred to Schelling's classic, *The Strategy of Conflict* [154]—but I shall limit myself to three basic aspects that have the greatest bearing on the practical question: What is the best thing to do about threats? To be successful, a threat must meet these conditions:

1. It must be convincing or believable enough to be taken seriously.
2. It must reach its target (the threatened party).
3. The target must be capable of complying with it.

If any one of these ingredients is missing or can be eliminated, the threat will fail.

How to make a threat stick, and how to unstick it

If somebody threatens to take you to court because you dropped a cigarette stub on his lawn, you will in all likelihood disregard it. If, on the other hand, somebody threatens to kill himself unless you let him eat your dessert *and* you know that this person has done crazy things in the past, you are likely to hand him your cake. In either case, the threat involves only a trivial matter, but while in the first instance the announced sanction seems absurd and the threat is therefore empty, the threat contained in the second example has a degree of credibility.

A threat is most effective if the threatener succeeds in engineering a situation in which the dire consequences, although originally created by him, are no longer under his control. One very common way of achieving this is to commit oneself so firmly to a course of action that one cannot be expected to withdraw from it without "loss of face"—an argument that carries very different weight in different cultures. The invocation of loss of face is particularly useful, since it is, in essence, intangible and can thus be made to mean or not mean a lot of things, all contrived to make the situation nonnegotiable.

There are also more tangible ways of proving that the threat is irreversible, such as reference to a power beyond one's reach whose commands cannot be changed or otherwise influenced. And strange as it may seem, one's own weakness can be exploited very compellingly—witness the coercion inherent in the disastrous economic situation of Great Britain and Italy, which forces the rest of the European countries to come to their rescue by massive loans lest the whole of the European community be dragged into bankruptcy. Very much the same kind of blackmail is part and parcel of most suicide threats and depressions, since few people are callous enough to shrug off the possibility of having contributed to somebody's disaster by ignoring his misery. In all these cases the threat is backed up by the plausible assertion "There is nothing I can do to stop or change it"—except that in these clinical cases the patient is totally unaware that he is making a threat and sincerely believes that he is only stating his discomfort and unhappiness. He thereby elicits the "helpful" attitude of relatives and friends who try to cheer him up by confident optimism, increased care and attention. The result of this is an interpersonal "game" played at ever-increasing stakes: by utilizing the dire threat of his helplessness, the patient blackmails the others into increased concern, and the more of this power he uses, the more the others respond. But once the solution of a human problem is based on this "more of the same" recipe [182], the only possible outcome is an escalation with potentially tragic consequences.

The very same mechanism can be used *against* the threatener. The most obvious and most widely used defense is a counterthreat of even greater seriousness and, therefore, believability. Here again, success depends upon an accurate evaluation of what will appear compelling in the other's (and not one's own) framework. The classic example from history is that of Cortez who, on arriving in what is today Veracruz, burned his ships and thereby precluded any pressure by his troops to be taken back to Spain, forcing them to conquer or perish. A more recent example is the Swiss response to Hitler's powerful threats to force them to yield control of their mountain passes and railways. By word and action they made it unmistakably clear that they would sacrifice their low-lying areas (population, industry, everything) and withdraw into the heavily fortified Alpine fortress, from which they could continue to block the strategic road and rail connections. Since the whole purpose of a German invasion of Switzerland would have been to gain control of the Alps and their passes, and since this was made to appear convincingly impossible, the invasion never took place. A similar philosophy underlies the presence of U.S. troops in Europe: the United States knows that the Soviets know that the United States knows that these troops are too few to represent a threat to the Warsaw Pact armies, but their physical presence represents a virtually nonnegotiable commitment by the United States not to yield to a military threat from the East.

The threat that cannot reach its target

It is obvious that a threat that cannot get through to or be understood by its target is ineffectual. The mad, the fanatic, the feeble-minded or young children may all be impervious to threats because they cannot (or pretend that they cannot) comprehend the implications. This is particularly noticeable with very young animals, which until a certain age get away with behavior for which an older animal would immediately be punished. There is a period when the group has to teach them, rather laboriously, the meaning of a threat.

It follows that one countermeasure against a threat is to make its receipt impossible. There are many ways in which this can be accomplished: by absent-mindedness, inattention, being deaf or drunk, avoiding a warning glance by looking in the other direction, claiming not to understand the language in which the threat is made, etc. Of course, here again the communication is interdependent: one's inability to receive the threat must be believable to the threatener; one must try to guess what the other, and not only oneself, will consider plausible and convincing.

Clever bank tellers sometimes manage to thwart a holdup in which a robber silently places a note in front of them, demanding that they fill a paper bag with money. Here the technique shifts from actual or pretended inability to understand the threat to a response for which the threatener is unprepared and which thereby "reframes" * the entire meaning of the situation. Almost any unexpected refusal may wreck the hoped-for sequence of events on which the robber based his *modus operandi* and thereby void his threat. Columnist Herb Caen once published a list of such refusals; here are some of them:

"You've got to be kidding!"
"I'm going to lunch now, please step to the next window."
"I don't have a bag, I'll have to get one."
"I'm sorry; I am a trainee and not allowed to handle cash—you'll have to wait for a regular teller." [30]

The cartoon on page 112 is based on the same idea.

The expedient of not letting a threat arrive at its target was seriously considered in the late sixties as a counter-measure against the increasing number of aerial hijackings. Basically, two very different procedures offered themselves. One was the method eventually chosen, security measures on the ground preventing the would-be hijackers from boarding the airliner. As we now know, these measures have gone far to eliminate air piracy, albeit through the creation of vast, elaborate and very expensive surveillance and screening procedures. The other method would have attempted to make air piracy impossible by completely

* For numerous examples of the concept of reframing as an important technique of problem resolution, see [186].

"I'm sorry, our bank went broke this morning."

separating the cockpit from the rest of the plane by a steel door and by switching off all other means of communication between the pilots and the cabin attendants. No matter what threats the hijacker made in the passenger cabin, the cabin attendants could convincingly prove to him that there was no way of informing the captain, and the plane would continue on its flight to its scheduled destination. The beauty of this solution would have been that the impenetrable separation of cockpit from passenger cabin not only would not have been kept a secret but would have been brought to the attention of the public by all available means. Unfortunately, this solution also has an insoluble drawback: no airline would be willing to run passenger flights under these circumstances, since there are dozens of incidents, from a smoldering fire in a toilet bin to a passenger's heart attack, that require immediate communication between passenger area and cockpit. However, the last word may not yet have been said about this subject, and the reader who succeeds in finding an ingenious way of utilizing the very special interdependent communication context between pirate and pilot may still be able to make a lot of money by selling his idea to the aviation authorities and the airlines.

Another technique is to create a situation of such confusion that the threat loses its power. The recent blackmail of the Hearst family (through the sensational but increasingly doubtful abduction of their daughter Patricia) provides an example of lost opportunities along this line. The abductors communicated with the family through notes and taped messages, which they played into the hands of the mass media. The media, true to their tradition of making the most out of anything sensational, rose to the occasion by treating these messages as if they were the word of God and immediately adopting the jargon of the abductors. They repeated that the girl was being held in a "people's prison" or referred—quite seriously and without quotation marks— to the head of the gang by his self-appointed rank of "General Field Marshal." While there was no way of preventing the abductors' threats from reaching their target (the family), their believability (and therefore their effectiveness) could have been largely destroyed if the investigating authorities had adapted some time-honored counterespionage techniques to this case. Utilizing the same channels of delivery as the abductors, it would have been relatively simple for them to deliver to the mass media fake messages, contradicting the real ones but similarly threatening the life of Patricia Hearst if they were not complied with. Very quickly a situation of total confusion could have been set up. None of the threats and demands could have been believed, because every message would have been contradicted or confused by another, allegedly coming from the "real" abductors and threatening dire consequences if the demands of the other group (perhaps described as a reactionary splinter faction which had broken its allegiance to the revolutionary cause and would soon meet with revolutionary justice) were met. Needless to say, in our era of alarming electronic progress, the production of perfectly genuine-sounding tapes would have presented no technical difficulties whatsoever. Once the confusion was created, it would then have been plausible for the family as well as the authorities to claim that they could not comply with any demand, since they had no way of telling the real from the fake ones. In other words, a reality would have been created *in which everything was false, and so was its contrary.* This is not only an old ploy in intelligence and especially in double-agent work, it is also an application of Erickson's Confusion Technique (pages 28–29) to a social context—except, of course, that the goal here is a different one.

The threat that cannot be obeyed

Even if a threat is believable and has reached its target, all is not necessarily lost. If I can convincingly show that I am unable to comply, the threat will be ineffective. For example, if somebody threatens my life unless I pay him a million dollars, I will have little difficulty proving to him that I do not have the money and could not possibly borrow or otherwise raise it. If, on the other hand, he only demands one hundred or even ten thousand dollars, I am in real trouble. Similarly, if terrorists abroad take a hostage on the mistaken assumption that he is an American citizen, his value as a hostage is zero, especially if he is the citizen of a small powerless country. Under these circumstances he need only point out to his abductors that the United States will ignore their threat and that his own government is not in the habit of rescuing its citizens who get into trouble.°

° That this may not work is borne out by the tragic fate of Guy Eid, the Egyptian-born chargé d'affaires at the Belgian embassy in Khartoum, killed by Al Fatah terrorists during their raid on the American embassy

The very receipt of a threat may at times precipitate a situation that makes compliance impossible. Fainting, a heart attack, an epileptic seizure—real or convincingly faked—puts not only the victim but also the threatener out of business. You *can* threaten to shoot an unconscious man if he does not comply, but it is not going to get you very far. And at least in theory, a death threat may be successfully countered if the victim has nerves of steel and manages to convince the threatener that he was on his way to commit suicide anyway, or that he has terminal cancer and has resigned himself to death.

Air travelers who pay attention to the demonstration of oxygen and other safety equipment may be surprised to hear the stewardess add an innocent-sounding statement: "Please notice that the rear door of our Boeing 727 can no longer be opened in flight." This simple modification was introduced after a rash of aerial hijackings in which pirates parachuted with the ransom money through the rear exit of 727s in flight, and put a quick end to this rather sporty technique. Again, it is significant that such a countermeasure must not only *not* be kept a secret but brought to the attention of as

---

on March 1, 1973, together with two U.S. diplomats, because the assassins mistook his identity and would not believe him when he said he was not an American.

Much less tragic was the fate of the wife of a French diplomat in bandit-infested China between the two world wars. As Daniele Varé reports this incident, the lady

> got caught by bandits in Manchuria, while I happened to be in Harbin. But she reappeared in town after a few days, having suffered no injury. We asked her how she had got away, and she said:
>
> "I went to the chief bandit and asked him if it were true that he meant to put me up to ransom at fifty thousand taels. He answered yes. So I said to him: 'Look at me. I never was beautiful. Now I am old and toothless. My husband wouldn't give five taels to get me back, let alone fifty thousand.' He saw the reasonableness of this argument and let me go." [173]

many people as possible. It is a good example of how a threat can be destroyed once and for all by an irreversible change of the physical circumstances on which it depends for its success.

Safeguards against threats are much more part and parcel of our lives than we realize. Schelling has pointed out that in democracies the secret ballot serves a similar function. It is not alone the secrecy, he writes,

> but the *mandatory* secrecy, that robs him [the voter] of his power. He not only *may* vote in secret, but he *must* if the system is to work. He must be denied any means of proving which way he voted. And what he is robbed of is not just an asset that he might sell; he is stripped of his power to be intimidated. He is made impotent to meet the demands of blackmail. There may be no limit to violence that he can be threatened with if he is truly free to bargain away his vote, since the threatened violence is not carried out anyway if it is frightening enough to persuade him. But when the voter is powerless to prove that he complied with the threat, both he and those who would threaten him know that any punishment would be unrelated to the way he actually voted. And the threat, being useless, goes idle. [157]

It is interesting to note that even the Nazis provided voting booths during their "elections," but that all true Nazis indignantly rejected this archaic carry-over from democratic days and cast their votes openly. The advantage was twofold: a flimsy appearance of secret voting was maintained, but anybody entering a voting booth to fill in his ballot was immediately suspected of casting a dissenting vote. This further discouraged dissenters and improved the always extraordinary election results. It is said that this convenient procedure is still practiced in some socialist countries, as it was in Greece under the Colonels' regime. Many police departments now have emergency squads, specially trained to handle abduction and extortion cases, the taking of hostages, etc., through the use of distractions, counterproposals, the clever invention of countless difficulties and circumstances beyond their control that delay the demanded course of action, the utilization of the psychological stress of the situation on the threateners themselves, and the deliberate use of misunderstanding and ambiguities.

Threats are as much a phenomenon of interdependence, as much aspects of specific patterns of communication as the structures we examined in the section on the Prisoner's Dilemma. Their mirror image is the promise, and I invite the reader to experiment with exchanging all the negative features of a threat for their opposites and thereby arrive at an understanding—both structural and pragmatic—of this aspect of interdependence.

13

Deception in Intelligence Work

Intelligence departments' work is generally considered to be twofold: to get information about the enemy (espionage) and to prevent the enemy from getting information (counterespionage).* There is also a third, much less well known task: feeding the enemy wrong information. This last function belongs under the heading of interdependence because the basic consideration remains, What does he think that I think that he thinks . . . , except that in this case the point is to make him think the *wrong* thing, to feed him a "wrong reality," and to take extreme care not to let him become aware of his mistaken assumptions until it is too

---

* There are, to be sure, other secret activities, usually of a nastier sort, such as sabotage and other special operations, but we are interested here only in information and disinformation.

late. The normal rules of communication are turned upside down, and disinformation becomes the ultimate goal.

The deception game was developed into a fine art by the British and German intelligence services during World War II. The Germans were particularly successful in what they called *Funkspiele* (wireless deception games). According to Walter Schellenberg, who was head of Amt VI (the German foreign political information service), they had at one time sixty-four captured Soviet wireless agents transmitting false information to Moscow [153].

The most comprehensive description of the British deception game is *The Double-Cross System in the War of 1939 to 1945*, by the historian and former member of the so-called Double-Cross Committee of the British Intelligence Service, Sir John C. Masterman [96], which was written in 1945 for very restricted circulation as a manual for future crises and released for general publication, virtually unchanged, in 1971. So incredibly successful were the British that there was not a single German spy in Great Britain during the war who was not under British control, although this became evident only toward the end of hostilities. "Being under British control" meant that these agents had either been apprehended by the British and "turned around," or had volunteered their services to the British while continuing to pose as German agents and reporting to their superiors in Germany.

In the topsy-turvy world of deliberate disinformation, the basic rule, to paraphrase Masterman, is that, rather than suppressing all enemy agents and thereby forcing the enemy to rebuild his spy nets, it is cheaper and more effective to "turn them around." °

° Popov, code-named Tricycle, one of the most successful British double agents, describes his exasperating experiences in this respect with the FBI in general and J. Edgar Hoover in particular. They were

This facilitates the detection of newly arrived agents, since they are usually instructed to contact an already identified spy; provides highly important insights into the enemy's *modus operandi;* and gives information about enemy codes and ciphers. The tasks assigned to these agents further reveal the nature and direction of the enemy's intentions. For example, when questions about ground and beach defenses stopped, the British concluded that the Germans had abandoned their plans to invade Great Britain. And by feeding the enemy the right kind of wrong but believable information through a turned-around agent, his plans can be influenced.

The last and perhaps most important function is defined by Masterman as follows:

> Finally, we are in a position to deceive the enemy. Clearly the necessity of sending information carries with it the power of misinformation, though it must be remembered that the force of this depends upon the reputation of the sender and that a long period of truthful reporting is usually a necessary preliminary for the passing over of the lie. [98]

We have already considered some of the effects paradoxical communications can have on the receiver's feelings of being "real." It is not surprising that a double agent suffers from a high degree of unreality, and the more real and convincing his deception, the more unreal he feels. If he is a turned-around spy, he is a prisoner of his captors, but to the other side he is an active, successful agent. And as long as his captors manage to guess correctly what their enemies will assume, this game can go on indefinitely until it becomes far more real than the spy himself. As long as his

interested only in arresting enemy agents, oblivious to the fact that the enemy would immediately replace them with new ones, who would have to be laboriously traced and arrested [131].

messages are believed to come from him, it does not matter whether he or his captors actually send them. Even if he is executed, he can continue to "exist" for the enemy. The ultimate refinement of this game is the so-called notional agent who, in Masterman's words, "never exists at all save in the minds or imagination of those who invented him and those who believe him" [97].° This is another striking example of those numerous communicational contexts "where validity depends on belief" [146].

Espionage establishments, of course, go to great lengths to protect themselves against this kind of deception. One relatively reliable safeguard lies in the fact that every wireless operator has his own distinctive style of using the wireless key, a kind of "fingerprint" that cannot easily be

---

° During the second half of 1943 the Allies suspected that German military intelligence (the Abwehr) was running a spy ring, composed of at least three agents, from Lisbon. The agents' code names were Ostro 1, Ostro 2 and Ostro 3, the first two operating in Britain, the third in the U.S.A. British intelligence sent crack agent Kim Philby (who later won world-wide notoriety when he defected to the Soviet Union in 1963) to Lisbon to investigate, and soon they knew more than the Abwehr about the Ostro agents and their spymaster, who had the somewhat weird code name Fidrmuc:

> Ostro was a magnificent hoax. Fidrmuc was operating alone. Ostro 1, 2, and 3 were ghosts. They were what is known in the trade as notional. Furthermore, Fidrmuc never did any actual spying. He based his reports on rumors, on what he could cull from periodicals, and foremost, on his fertile imagination. And for this he milked the Abwehr royally and ingeniously, accepting only part payment in cash, the rest being in art objects, which he sold at a high profit. [132]

Since there was a real danger that Fidrmuc's inventions could one day come dangerously close to the truth or discredit the information the British wanted the Germans to believe, he was eliminated by passing on to the Germans information whose truth they could verify which contradicted Fidrmuc's reports.

imitated and is as distinguishable to an expert as the use of a musical instrument by a particular artist. Furthermore, agents who send their messages by wireless are usually instructed to omit a certain group of three or five letters (the "security check") at the beginning of any message if they are caught and turned around. The absence of these letters is supposed to warn the receiver: "I am captured; don't believe my messages any more."

A remarkable human shortcoming is, however, likely to interfere with these and other simple precautions. We have already encountered it when discussing the stubbornness with which creatures adhere to the belief systems created by random reward experiments. People are very reluctant to give up confidence in their laboriously constructed views of reality, even when it turns out that there is no connection between their performance and their rewards. Similarly in intelligence work; so much thinking and planning, so many hopes and fears have gone into the making of an agent's fictional identity, his training, his particular mission and his eventual dispatch into enemy territory that even supposedly cool-headed and dispassionate planners of intelligence missions get caught up in their own game, both intellectually and emotionally, and are unable to see what they do not want to see. Masterman writes:

> It was extremely, almost fantastically, difficult to "blow" a well-established agent. On one occasion an agent was deliberately run in order to show the Germans that he was under control, the object being to give them a false idea of our methods of running such an agent and thus to convince them that the other agents were genuine. The theory was sound and the gaffes committed were crass and blatant, but the object was not achieved, for the simple reason that the Germans continued to think of the agent as being genuine and reliable! [99]

The British were not at all immune to this kind of thinking either, as the *Englandspiel* [161], also known under the code name Operation North Pole, shows. Fifty-three of their agents were parachuted in and were arrested, one after the other, on their arrival in German-occupied Holland, and turned around. The first one who was caught correctly omitted to send the "security check," but London ignored this, probably because the directors of the operation were too delighted with their "success." The Germans exploited the situation to the hilt, requesting the dispatch of (and immediately taking into custody) agent after agent and substantial quantities of matériel.° At long last London grew suspicious, and when eventually three of the turned-around agents managed to escape from German custody, and warn London, the Germans had no way of continuing the deception. Their last message to London read:

> We are aware of the fact that for some time you have been doing business in Holland without our help. Since we have been your only representatives for a long time, we find this rather unfair. However, this does not exclude the fact that, should you decide to pay us a visit on a larger scale, you will receive the same hospitality as your agents. [163]

As everybody knows, the Allies did eventually pay "a visit on a larger scale," but the hospitality worked the other way around.

Another remarkable impasse arises in deception games when enemy agents defect. They usually come well supplied with all kinds of intelligence gems about their own

° All in all, the British obligingly parachuted into Holland 570 containers and 150 packages containing 15,200 kilograms of explosives, 3,000 Sten guns, 5,000 pistols and numerous other matériel, as well as 500,000 Dutch guilders [162].

service and its operations. Under normal circumstances, the arrival of such a defector provides a welcome windfall, and depending on the amount and quality of his information, may enable the other side to detect entire espionage systems. But in the strange upside-down world of the double-agent system, in which the signs of all communications are reversed, exactly the opposite is the case, and the defection may cause a major catastrophe: the defector's own country knows, of course, how much the defector knows. Since he has information on many of its spies, these agents are likely to be rounded up and put out of action. This means that those enemy agents who are really double agents are made useless by the defection, for if they continued to send messages, the enemy would realize that there was something fishy about them.

Another unusual problem arises in the case of the double-agent saboteur. If he is ordered by the enemy to carry out an act of sabotage, he cannot simply send in a fictitious report, since in all likelihood other agents, unknown to him, will be instructed to make an independent check on the action and assess its success. It is also very difficult to prevent reports of major explosions, etc., from being reported in the press. If the enemy espionage system (one of whose functions is a careful analysis of the other side's news media) cannot find any reference to the reported sabotage, this will create suspicion. Something *must* happen to make the double-agent saboteur believable in the eyes of the enemy, and this something has to be big enough to be reported in the news media. This is not an easy matter; one cannot very well blow up one's country's bridges or factories just to create a good impression in the enemy's eyes. One such operation, carried out by the British in 1941 and code-named Plan Guy Fawkes, involved arranging a minor explosion in a food dump near London. Masterman describes the almost slapstick nature of this top-secret enterprise:

> In this particular case a high official at the Ministry of Food had to be taken into our confidence, as well as the Commissioner of Police at Scotland Yard, but even so there were many ticklish moments before the operation was successfully completed. The two aged fire guards at the food store could only with difficulty be roused from slumber and lured away from that part of the premises where the incendiary bomb had been placed. A too zealous local policeman almost succeeded in arresting our officers, and it was a matter of great difficulty to ensure that the fire resulting from the explosion should be sufficiently fierce to cause excitement in the district and yet not great enough to cause serious damage before the fire brigades could overcome it. [100]

One of the minor delights of double agents' work must be the fact that it is paid for by the enemy. But it is also a source of worry, because if no money arrives, the agents cannot continue to function in a way that is believable to the other side. (A bona fide German agent who was parachuted into England reportedly committed suicide for this reason; he did not receive his money and had nowhere to turn.) In World War II, the survival of at least a few neutral, unoccupied countries like Spain, Portugal and Sweden made money transactions possible. Some British double agents received regular payments from Germany through an arrangement whereby Spanish fruit importers in England made these payments to them (or rather to the British intelligence service) in return for equivalent sums paid by the Abwehr in pesetas to these firms in Spain.

But perhaps even more important is the necessity to provide agents on enemy soil with the tools of their trade. In double-agent work this provides an elegant opportunity to have the enemy deliver, free of charge, specimens of just about anything in his intelligence armamentarium: codes and new coding procedures, transmitters, forgeries revealing the latest state of the art, sabotage gadgets, surveillance equipment and many other things of the highest importance for planning espionage and counterespionage activities.

Under the peculiar communication contexts of double-agent work, it is possible to create almost any kind of "reality" in the enemy's mind, provided the deception contains just enough truth, or at least probability, to be believable. One can, for instance, leak to the enemy false information about the development of a new weapons system and thereby greatly influence his armament programs or combat tactics. In the years preceding World War II a persistent rumor circulated throughout Europe: in a certain area, close to a German military testing ground, all motor vehicles would periodically stall. As the drivers looked under the hoods for the cause, an SS man would appear and tell them not to bother, because in half an hour their cars would be running again. Sure enough, exactly at the predicted time all the cars started again without difficulty. We now know that no such secret weapon was ever developed, but the rumor helped support the idea that great things were in the making.

Sometimes a rumor may start inadvertently and become the object of tenacious espionage efforts. Between March and June 1942 the Germans tried five times to obtain information on what they referred to as the "crusher" tank. No such tank was under development by the Allies, and they had no idea what the Germans were looking for. At the height of the Cold War period, the Soviets leaked information to the West, disguised as eyewitness accounts of a gigantic and frightening experiment during which, by some secret device, the atmospheric temperature was precipitously lowered and a whole lake frozen over in the middle of summer.°

Operation Mincemeat

On April 30, 1943, the body of a major in the Royal Marines was picked up by fishermen off the Spanish port of Huelva on the Atlantic Coast. Documents and other corroborative evidence found on his person left no doubt that he was a courier on his way from London to Eighteenth Army General Headquarters in Tunisia and that his plane had crashed into the sea.

When the Spanish authorities investigating the case managed to extract several official letters found on the body, without breaking the seals of the envelopes, they immediately realized that these were documents of the highest military importance. There was a letter from the Vice-Chief of the Imperial General Staff to General Alexander, the Deputy Commander to General Eisenhower in North Africa, dealing with various matters related to the Mediterranean campaign and rather carelessly hinting at Greece as one of two invasion targets. Another, more personal letter from Admiral Mountbatten to Admiral Cunningham, the commander in chief of the Allied naval forces in the Mediterranean, also contained very definite suggestions to this effect.

Almost immediately the British vice-consul in Huelva and the British naval attaché in Madrid began inquiries about the case, at first very discreetly and then more and more openly, with the obvious aim of having the body and all the

---

° Of course, any such ploy may backfire very badly if in addition to frightening the other side, it also propels it into yet greater paranoia and armaments escalation.

documents handed over to them. The Spaniards stalled long enough to enable the German espionage agent in Huelva to squeeze the last bit of information out of this fantastic intelligence windfall, then replaced the letters in their envelopes and complied with the British request. There is a simple gravestone in the cemetery of Huelva with the inscription "William Martin. Born 29th March 1907. Died 24th April 1943. Beloved son of John Glyndwyr Martin and the late Antonia Martin of Cardiff, Wales. *Dulce et decorum est pro patria mori*. R.I.P."

In point of fact, Major William Martin never existed. The creation of this fictitious person was probably the most successful deception game of World War II, code-named Operation Mincemeat. Since a detailed account of the operation has been published by its main architect, Lieutenant Commander Ewen Montagu in *The Man Who Never Was* [104], I shall highlight only a few seemingly minor communicational ploys that are directly relevant to our subject matter.

After the Allied occupation of the North African coast in 1943, preparations got under way for a landing on what Churchill called "the soft underbelly of Europe"—Sicily. Any such operation involves an interdependent decision procedure in reverse, so to speak; that is, while normally the outcome of decision making should be agreement and coordination, here the desired goal was deception and confusion. The Allied strategists had to answer the question: What will the Germans think that we think is the best target? A look at the map shows there were three possible answers: Greece, Sicily and Sardinia. Of the three, Sicily was by far the closest and most important target. This being so, the most reasonable course of action for the Axis high commands was to fortify the southern and eastern coast of the island and commit the bulk of their troops to its defense—*unless* they received plausible information that precisely because an assault on Sicily was so obvious, the Allies were planning to land elsewhere.°

For the Allies the crucial question was: What would constitute plausible information for the German high command? In any communication context, the reliability of information depends on two factors: the probability of the information itself and the credibility of its source. Information that contradicts known facts has a very low probability rating. Information that comes from a notoriously unreliable source, or from a source whose reliability cannot be assessed because no or very little information has so far been received from it, or from a source that could not conceivably come into possession of such information, is considered unbelievable. For the planners of Operation Mincemeat this meant:

First, the information put into the Germans' hands had to make sense within *their* frame of reference and the information available to *them*, not necessarily in the British perspective. Very much as in other interdependent decisions, success depended on evaluating correctly what seemed right to the Germans (not to the Allies) and what *they* thought the Allies were thinking. Of course, once important information comes into the enemy's hands, he is bound to look for confirmation which, to quote Montagu, means that

> you must think out what enquiries will *he* make (not what enquiries would *you* make) and give him the answers to those enquiries so as to satisfy him. In other words, you must

° Decision making under these or similar circumstances quickly acquires some of the characteristics of a *prediction paradox:* The more likely an opponent's action seems, the less likely it becomes; but the less likely it becomes, the more likely it is that the opponent will resort to it. (More on this type of communication paradox can be found in reference 179.)

remember that a German does not think and react as an Englishman does, and you must put yourself into his mind. [106]

Ironically, it turned out to be more difficult for the planners to get this crucial point into the heads of their own superiors than to deceive the Germans.°

° Over a hundred years ago, Edgar Allan Poe masterfully depicted a very similar interdependent decision in reverse. In "The Purloined Letter" his detective Dupin manages to find a stolen letter that is of the utmost importance to the Prefect of Paris. The Prefect knows that it is hidden in the apartment of his adversary D., but even the most careful search by his secret agents fails to bring it to light. In his explanation of how he solved the case, Dupin points to exactly the same necessity that Montagu had to face and that he found so difficult to make his superiors appreciate. The Prefect's agents, Poe writes,

consider only their *own* ideas of ingenuity; and, in searching for anything hidden, advert only to the modes in which *they* would have hidden it. They are right in this much—that their own ingenuity is a faithful representative of that of *the mass;* but when the cunning of the individual felon is diverse in character from their own, the felon foils them, of course. This always happens when it is above their own, and very usually when it is below. They have no variation of principle in their investigations; at best, when urged by some unusual emergency— by some extraordinary reward—they extend or exaggerate their old modes of *practice,* without touching their principles. What, for example, in this case of D., has been done to vary the principle of action? What is all this boring, and probing, and sounding, and scrutinizing with the microscope, and dividing the surface of the building into registered square inches—what is it all but an exaggeration *of the application* of the one principle or set of principles of search, which are based upon the one set of notions regarding human ingenuity, to which the Prefect, in the long routine of his duty, has been accustomed? Do you not see he has taken it for granted that *all* men proceed to conceal a letter—not exactly in a gimlet-hole bored in a chair-leg—but, at least, in *some* out-of-the-way hole or corner suggested by the same tenor of thought which would urge a man to secrete a letter in a gimlet-hole bored in a chair-leg?

Second, as far as the reliability of the source was concerned, it was clear that the Germans would not believe a decision of such strategic importance and fateful consequences if the information emanated from a minor source or was a mere report from such a source. Only a convincing leak in the highest echelons of the Allied Supreme Command would do—for instance, a document that without doubt came direct from such a source. This immediately ruled out information received through the more customary channels of intelligence gathering, such as an agent, a prisoner of war or a deserter; none of these sources could ever be in possession of such top-level information.°

Operation Mincemeat managed to satisfy both these preconditions:

1. The planners first asked themselves how much the Germans could be expected to know about the logistics of an amphibious assault involving large numbers of men and matériel across a relatively wide body of water. It seemed probable that they knew very little and were thus not in a good position to distinguish fact from fiction. Moreover, Allied air superiority in the Mediterranean prevented them from acquiring crucial intelligence, above all the number of landing craft and other shipping available to the Allies. It

---

On the strength of Dupin's correct evaluation of what D. thought that the Prefect's agents thought that D. was thinking, Dupin has no difficulty spotting the letter in a very unsecret place, namely "in a card-rack of paste-board, that hung dangling by a dirty blue ribbon, from a little brass knob just beneath the middle of the mantle-piece."

° There are occasional exceptions to this rule. One was Ilya Basna, code-named Cicero by the Germans, the valet of the British ambassador in Ankara. He simply helped himself to the key of the embassy safe while his master was asleep and supplied the Germans with the most secret and detailed information, including the minutes of the Teheran Conference. He was royally rewarded with the equivalent of one and a half million dollars in British pound notes, most of which, alas, had a minor flaw: they were counterfeit.

therefore seemed reasonable that they could be made to believe that the two Allied armies in North Africa could mount two separate, simultaneous assaults against Greece and Sardinia—a strategic feat the Allies could actually have accomplished only with the help of Santa Claus.

To make the deception even more plausible to the Germans and to provide additional cover for the real operation (the invasion of Sicily), the planners of Operation Mincemeat included in the information leak the hint that they were going to convince the Germans that Sicily was their real target. The beauty of this additional wrinkle (a metadeception, so to speak) was that as a result, any real leakage about the real invasion plan (which in view of its magnitude seemed virtually unavoidable) would now appear to be a deliberate plant and convince the enemy even more firmly that the "secret" intelligence in his possession was correct. To make this still more believable, the code name of the real invasion plan for Sicily, "Husky," was alleged to be the code name for the (fictitious) invasion of Greece. Thus, if German agents were ever to come across "Husky," they would be further confirmed in their belief that Greece was one of the two targets (the other being Sardinia).°

2. The next question was how this believable information could be believably played into the hands of the German high command. Invasion plans don't just lie around waiting to be picked up by spies; they are most carefully guarded, and nothing short of an act of God or some major security disaster makes them accessible to outsiders. Furthermore,

---

° The reader will notice that this situation is the mirror image of the "therapy session" between Dr. Jackson and the clinical psychologist (pages 84–85). There the context was such that the more sanity each partner tried to inject into the situation, the crazier he appeared to the other. Here the converse was the case: the more the truth was presented as a deception, the more believable the deception became.

the information had to be planted in such a way that it could safely be expected to get into the "right" hands and at the same time lost and recovered by the Allies under circumstances that "justified" them in "believing" that it could *not* have become known to the enemy—for no strategist in his right mind would go ahead with a plan he has reason to suspect has become known to the enemy. The Spanish and German intelligence services kindly made this possible by taking great pains not to arouse British suspicion, making the letters appear untouched and returning them with the corpse to the British authorities without undue delay. In other words, they played their expected role in the deception game, being deceived while believing that they were deceiving. And thus, as so often happens in deception contexts, two "wrongs" did make a "right."

The success of Operation Mincemeat exceeded the hopes of its planners. In Montagu's own words:

> As regards the Eastern Mediterranean: we caused immense effort to be put into the defence of Greece, with the creation of minefields, shore batteries, etc.; we caused a concentration of troops in Greece which justified the appointment by Hitler of Rommel to command them; these troops included a panzer division which had to be sent right across Europe; all this was completely wasted effort from the German point of view and diminished the potential defence of Sicily and of Italy.
>
> As regards the Western Mediterranean: we caused an increase in the fortification and reinforcement of Corsica and Sardinia at the expense of that of Sicily; we caused the defensive preparations in Sicily to be largely diverted from these coasts of the island where the Allies in fact landed to the coasts where they did not land; we caused the Germans to send R-boats away from Sicily to the Aegean, thus opening a gap in their defences which "prejudiced the defence of Sicily" as well as creating a shortage of escort vessels. [108]

These results first became apparent from intelligence reports and were confirmed objectively when the secret documents of the German high command were opened after the war. The Allies had succeeded in creating a totally false "reality."

This is where a brief description of Operation Mincemeat should properly end, but I cannot resist the temptation of listing a few of the minor problems that surfaced in the course of its execution, admittedly not because they add much to this book, but because they have a macabre charm of their own.

First of all, there had to be a body whose cause of death was at least not in flagrant contradiction with the results of an airplane crash. A suitable corpse was found as early as January 1943 and had to be kept on ice until it was launched from a British submarine off Huelva in April. (The true identity of the deceased was never revealed.)

While there was little difficulty in getting a complete military outfit for the body, it proved extremely complicated to find underwear, since this required rationing coupons and the rationing authorities could not possibly be let in on a top-secret matter. Eventually a private gift solved the problem.

Has any reader tried to dress a frozen corpse? Montagu and his assistant found that it can be done—except for the boots. One simply cannot slip them over feet that are sticking out rigidly at right angles to the leg. At considerable risk, the feet had to be thawed and quickly frozen again.

This led to another problem: the credibility of the body's condition from a pathologist's point of view. After thawing and floating for a number of days in relatively warm water, would its physical state not reveal that it had been dead for months? An eminent pathologist, Sir Bernard Spillsbury, was confidentially consulted in this matter, and unencumbered by false modesty, came to the conclusion: "You have nothing to fear from a Spanish *post mortem;* to detect that this young man did not die after an aircraft had been lost at sea would need a pathologist of my experience—and there aren't any in Spain" [105].

To add to the plausibility of the entire deception, Major Martin's death was duly reported in *The Times* of June 4, 1943, so that German intelligence (known to study British papers very carefully as soon as they arrived in Lisbon, Madrid, Stockholm, etc.) would find further "evidence" of his genuineness. But this caused unexpected trouble at home: "The Naval Wills Department wanted to know whether he had made a will—and if so, where was it? The Medical Director General's Department wanted to know whether Maj. Martin had been killed in action, died of wounds, died on active service, or what, so that their statistics could be kept in order" [107]. It took a good deal of additional deception, for domestic consumption, to set these bureaucratic minds at ease.

When German documents became available after the war, it turned out that in spite of its meticulous planning, Operation Mincemeat could easily have gone awry as a result of certain mistakes committed by the *Germans,* not the British! When the photographed documents were translated into German, several dates were copied incorrectly, thereby making the carefully prepared chronology of the events supposedly preceding and leading up to the "plane crash" very unlikely. But the Germans somehow failed to notice these rather glaring inconsistencies. Again, two wrongs made a right; once a deception is swallowed, fantastic blind spots are likely to develop for evidence to the contrary. And this leads into another famous disinformation game, Operation Neptune.

Operation Neptune

Actually, Neptune was not so much a deception game in the sense just described as what in Soviet-bloc intelligence lingo is called an *influence operation*. Unlike the Western intelligence services, the Soviet bloc distinguishes between three main forms of deception: disinformation, propaganda and influence operations. The first, disinformation, is virtually identical with what has been described in the preceding pages; propaganda hardly requires definition; influence operations are covert actions, utilizing existing political or social trends or quite unsuspecting prominent personalities (so-called useful idiots) in the target country for specific purposes. The riots in Panama in January 1964 are a good example—ostensibly they were a spontaneous outburst of youthful Latin-American nationalism against U.S. imperialism; covertly they appear to have been carefully engineered by, of all people, agents of the Czechoslovak intelligence service normally operating in Mexico [20].

Operation Neptune was also a product of Czechoslovak intelligence. It took place during the spring of 1964, and its purpose was threefold: to rally public opinion throughout Europe against the then imminent expiration of the statute of limitations for war crimes in West Germany; to rekindle resentment and anti-German feelings by presenting to the public supposedly new facts about Nazi atrocities; and to launch a piece of disinformation, intended to interfere with West German intelligence operations, by making public the names of Czechoslovak citizens who had collaborated with the Germans during the war and could be assumed to be still working for the intelligence services of the Federal Republic of Germany.

Ever since the end of World War II there had been

discoveries of documents, stolen art treasures, war chests and the like throughout Europe, especially in the area that had still been under German control immediately before the surrender. How true it is that plans for hiding important archives were actually elaborated during a high-level conference of Nazi officials in Strasbourg on August 10, 1943, is not certain, but at least some caches of documents were constructed in great secrecy and elaborately concealed, obviously in order to have them handy when the Fourth Reich was born. Tales of former German soldiers secretly trying to recover hidden treasures kept making the rounds in those years and gained world-wide attention when some experimental German navy equipment and several cases of homemade British currency (of the kind Cicero was paid with) were found by Austrian authorities at the bottom of Lake Toplitz near Bad Aussee. The case had come to the attention of the police after a German "tourist" accidentally lost his life while skin-diving in the lake.

Although this incident took place in 1959, persistent rumor had it that in the border regions of Upper Austria, Bavaria and Bohemia, the bottoms of lakes, abandoned mines and the vaults of old castles contained important wartime documents as well as fabulous treasures.

Not surprisingly, the world was electrified in late May 1964 when the Czechoslovak authorities announced that their intelligence service had recovered four large, asphalt-covered cases from the Black Lake near Sušice in southern Bohemia. Thanks to the defection of one of the planners of this operation, Ladislav Bittman, we now know that these cases had been prepared and thrown into the lake by the Czechoslovak intelligence service a few weeks prior to their sensational discovery by a television crew that "happened" to be shooting underwater pictures in the lake. With special secrecy precautions, designed to attract public attention, the cases were taken to Prague, and eventually both their contents and the film of their discoveries were made public at a press conference. Operation Neptune was considered a great success.

But was it? According to Bittman, it was really a rather mediocre job. Early on there was a security leak which nearly ended the project. Furthermore, after the recovery of the cases from the lake, the planners of the operation still could not decide which documents had purportedly been found in them. There was little in the Czechoslovak archives that was not already known to historians, but Moscow had promised to let them have hitherto unpublished German documents from their files. These arrived less than a week before the press conference and turned out to be something of a disappointment: not only did some of the documents have notations in Cyrillic on them, they were a hodge-podge, apparently pulled together from very different sources. Among other information, they contained reports on an investigation into the causes of the failure of the Nazi putsch in Austria in July 1934; some Italian documents relating, of all things, to the dispatch of German agents from Italy to Latin America; some reports of very local importance on German military intelligence operations in France after the landing in Normandy; several war diaries of German army units operating on the eastern front; and other heterogeneous material. Why this motley collection should have been put together in the first place, coming from such totally disparate sources as the army, the SS Historical Commission, and the Reichssicherheitshauptamt (Himmler's intelligence organization, which had eventually taken over Admiral Canaris' Abwehr); what sort of unit would carry such stuff around, and why it should have been preserved for posterity, was never explained.

Yet in spite of these glaring shortcomings, Operation Neptune was swallowed without a murmur, showing that the content of communications is relatively unimportant compared to the recipient's readiness to believe them, either because they fit into his belief system or because of the context in which they are presented. Few believers in the authenticity of the *Protocols of the Elders of Zion* ever felt the need to read them, few devoted Nazis worked their way through *Mein Kampf,* and not many Americans more than skimmed through the *Pentagon Papers.* But the fact that this was so did not prevent people from taking passionate and vociferous stands for or against these revelations.

However, despite the public splash it received, Operation Neptune's practical effects appear to have been negligible. Not only did the documents reveal nothing particularly new, the planners fell victim to their own (Soviet bloc) propaganda, which consistently equates the Federal Republic of Germany with Nazi Germany, expecting that everybody else would do so too. Here, then, is an example of decision making based on an erroneous "what we think that they think that we think . . ." evaluation of interdependence.

14

The Two Realities

Having arrived at the end of Part II, it seems useful to put some order into the kaleidoscopic diversity of the preceding examples and to show that they have an important common denominator.

The reader will have noticed that I have been unable to avoid the use of terms like "really," "actually," "in actual fact," and thus have apparently contradicted the main thesis of the book: that there is no absolute reality but only subjective and often contradictory conceptions of reality.

Very frequently, especially in psychiatry where the degree of an individual's "reality adaptation" plays a special role as the indicator of his normalcy, there is a confusion between two very different aspects of what we call reality. The first has to do with the purely physical, objectively discernible properties of things and is intimately linked with correct sensory perception, with questions of so-called common sense or with objective, repeatable, scientific verification. The second aspect is the attribution of meaning and value to these things and is based on communication.

For example, before the advent of space travel there was heated disagreement among astronomers as to whether the surface of the moon was solid enough to support the weight of a space probe or whether it was covered by a thick layer of dust that would completely swallow the craft. We now know that the first hypothesis is *really* the case and that some scientists were therefore objectively right and others wrong. Or, to use a much simpler example, the question of whether a whale is a fish or a mammal can be answered objectively, as long as there is agreement on the definitions of "fish" and "mammal." Let us, therefore, use the term first-order reality whenever we mean those aspects which are accessible to perceptual consensus and especially to experimental, repeatable and verifiable proof (or refutation).

This domain of reality, however, says nothing about the *meaning* and *value* of its contents. A small child may perceive a red traffic light just as clearly as an adult, but may not know that it means "do not cross the street now." The first-order reality of gold—that is, its physical properties—is known and can be verified at any time. But the role that gold has played since the dawn of human history, especially the fact that its value is determined twice daily by five men in a small office in the City of London and that this ascription of value profoundly influences many other aspects of our everyday reality, has very little, if anything, to do with the physical properties of gold. But it is this second reality of gold which may turn us into millionaires or lead us into bankruptcy.

The interpersonal conflicts mentioned in preceding chapters, those caused by the discrepancy of cultural roles and norms, show the difference between the two orders of reality even more sharply. Quite obviously, there is no such thing as an objectively "correct" distance between two people, and depending on the norms of a given culture, kissing may be "correct" either in the early or only in the final stages of courtship behavior. Such rules are subjective, arbitrary and have nothing to do with the expression of eternal, Platonic truths. In the domain of second-order reality then, it is absurd to argue about what is "really" real.

But we lose sight of this distinction all too easily, or, worse, we are totally unaware of the existence of two very separate realities and naïvely assume that reality is the way we see things, and anybody who sees them differently must of necessity be mad or bad.

It can be objectively verified if I jump in the water to save a drowning person. But there is no objective evidence as to whether I do it out of charity, the need to appear heroic, or because I know that the drowning man is a millionaire. On these questions there are only subjective attributions of meaning. It is a delusion to believe that there is a "real" second-order reality and that "sane" people are more aware of it than "madmen."

PART III
Communication

> *Thus it is a property of man to*
> *be capable of learning grammar.*

> —Aristotle, *Topica* I 5, 102a 20

In everything we have considered thus far there has always been the precondition of communication; the problems that arose were all due to various circumstances that impeded the *exchange* of information. Once this impediment was lifted, communication could flow freely. For example, once an interpreter is found, a bridge can be established between two different languages, because these two languages already exist and can be translated into each other, especially since they are both used by human beings for almost identical purposes and under almost identical environmental conditions. Similarly, paradoxes can be resolved, if necessary by recourse to counterparadoxes based on the same general logic. Clever Hans used existing clues that were obvious to him, even though they were not to his experimenters. Two people caught in the Prisoner's Dilemma are both aware of the payoffs; the blackmailer and his victim speak the same language. And a successful piece of intelligence disinformation is based on a painstaking evaluation of the opponent's sense of conceptualizing reality (i.e., of his second-order reality) and of his goals within the limits and possibilities of a physical universe shared by both sides (i.e., their first-order reality).

What follows now is quite different. It deals with contexts in which the shared basis of communication does not yet exist but has to be invented and then offered to the other side in such a way that the other side will be able to discover its meaning. That is, the problems involved here are concerned with laying the basis for an information exchange, and only secondarily with the exchange itself. But once this exchange is established, it may reveal to both sides the most unexpected and unimaginable insights into the second-order reality of their partners.

This will bring us in contact with two of mankind's oldest dreams: communication with animals and with extraterrestrial beings. As far as animals are concerned, we shall see that very interesting progress has been made (without falling back into the Clever Hans mistake) toward the elaboration of languages which both the human and his animal partner can share.

Communication with extraterrestrial beings may cease to be a dream within the lifetime of my younger readers, thanks to the fantastic advances of science. Of course, our interest will focus only very little on the technical aspects. We shall consider mainly the question of how to establish a common ground of understanding with these beings once technology has made communication a practical possibility. We shall see that the problems to be solved there are again of a very basic, almost timeless nature.

Finally we shall enter yet another field, one that many of my readers may refuse to associate with communication at all but which, it seems to me, does enter into the more esoteric aspects of communications research and at the same time will steadily grow in importance as science becomes less and less directly accessible to common sense. We shall again merely scrape the surface of a vast and uncharted territory, limiting ourselves to a few examples of the very intriguing problems arising out of purely imaginary interactions with imaginary beings or in imaginary situations.

15

The Chimpanzee

Of all our close cousins in the animal kingdom, none seems so human as the chimpanzee. However, while some close physiological similarities do exist, and while much of the chimp's social behavior has striking affinities with our own, this closeness can be very misleading and blind us to the profound differences between them and us. Anybody watching chimpanzee behavior—their movements, emotional manifestations, the expressiveness of their faces—is tempted to conclude that if taught to speak, they would be practically our equals. And indeed they are quite adept at learning to *understand* our language—but so is the dog and several other higher mammals.

As a matter of fact, the history of man-chimpanzee relations is fairly rich in attempts to teach the animal our language. These experiments have usually involved raising very young chimps in homes under circumstances identical to those under which a human infant is brought up. The most widely known and probably best-documented attempt of this kind was made by two members of the Yerkes Laboratories of Primate Biology in Florida, Keith and Catherine Hayes [62, 63].° Like several other researchers, they found that the chimpanzee's ability to acquire and use human language was extremely limited. Their little ward,

---

° A more popularly written account is Catherine Hayes's book *The Ape in Our House* [59], which contains a wealth of charming and revealing incidents. Two in particular give an insight into the chimp's gentle nature and potential for sharing reality—even an imaginary reality.

The young chimp Viki sometimes played with dogs and cats. On one occasion a cat she knew was sick and was sunning itself on the back steps of a neighbor's house. "Viki glanced at it now and then and finally she went over to it. The cat did not move. Viki bent over from the waist and looked into its face. Then she kissed it and quietly went away" [61].

On another occasion Viki invented an imaginary pull toy; that is, she behaved as if she were pulling a string with a toy attached to it all around the bathroom. Eventually she elaborated this game to the point where she pretended that the string had become entangled and she was unable to extricate her imaginary toy. She looked up at Mrs. Hayes and called loudly, "Mama! Mama!"

Suddenly I was frightened by the eerie quality of the whole business, but I felt that I must play along for the sake of our future harmony. I said with a smile, "Here, let me help you."

Acting out an elaborate pantomime I took the rope from her hands and, with much pulling and manipulation, untangled it from the plumbing. I dared not meet her eyes until I held out to her the rope which neither of us could see (I think). "Here you are, little one," I said.

Then I saw the expression on her face. In a human mute it might have been called a look of sheer devotion, of appreciation for understanding. In addition a tiny smile played on her lips. And her whole face reflected the wonder in children's faces when they are astonished at a grownup's enthusiastic escape into make-believe. [60]

A shared benign delusion or shadows of Clever Hans across half a century?

Viki, lived in their house for six years, but in spite of being exposed as extensively to human speech as a young child of the same age, and in spite of understanding many commands, she never managed to say more than four words: "mama," "papa," "cup" and "up." Even these words were very difficult for her to pronounce, and she often used them incorrectly.

Viki's failure seemed to confirm the traditional view that only humans are capable of generating and learning a language that goes beyond the vocalization of emotions, warning cries, and the like, and incorporates such complex achievements as the use of symbols or arbitrarily chosen sounds (words) to denote objects and concepts, to form sentences and to rearrange them into novel combinations. As the epigraph to this chapter shows, this view has been held since the days of Aristotle. We have since learned, however, that as far as chimpanzees are concerned, their inability to acquire speech is mostly anatomical: they simply do not possess a sufficiently differentiated sound-producing organ. As Robert Yerkes and Blanche Learned noted fifty years ago, their otherwise remarkable imitative tendencies do not include sounds: "I have never heard them imitate a sound and rarely make a sound peculiarly their own in response to mine" [191].

Their hands, however, are extremely well developed and give them great dexterity. To appreciate this one has only to watch them at the zoo or read Jane van Lawick-Goodall's charming book *In the Shadow of Man* [86] and examine the photographs in it. There is now well-documented evidence that chimpanzees have a wide variety of communicative gestures (greeting, begging, embracing, kissing, reassuring, playing) which look amazingly "human," and also that they very adroitly use certain tools and are able to improvise new ones as the need arises. In recent years a number of researchers have therefore turned to languages that use the hands and other parts of the body. These languages have the enormous advantage that, unlike speech, they can easily be shared by humans and all of the great apes. Even at this relatively early stage one is left with the impression that King Solomon's ring has at last been found, or that, to put it a little less enthusiastically, the Clever Hans trauma has at last been overcome. Very promising results have already been achieved.

Sign language

In June 1966 Allen and Beatrice Gardner, both psychologists at the University of Nevada in Reno, began to work with a wild-born female chimpanzee who was then approximately a year old, whom they called Washoe. Their object was to establish communication by means of American Sign Language (ASL) and test to what extent this could become a medium of communication between humans and apes [47, 56].

Like other sign languages developed by and for the use of deaf people, ASL has a vocabulary of 5,000–10,000 signs, based mostly on hand, arm and head gestures. Many of these signs are quite representational or iconic; that is, the particular gesture bears a direct relation to what it denotes. For example, the sign for "flower" is exactly the gesture anybody would perform when holding a bud in his fingers, bringing it to his nose and sniffing at it first with one, then the other nostril. Other signs are more arbitrary; "shoes," for instance, is signed by striking the sides of one's fisted hands against each other. By and large, however, all signs are to a certain degree mixtures of iconic and arbitrary elements, and very much as in other pictorial languages, a great deal of blurring and simplification occurs through constant use. Incidentally, to anybody unfamiliar with sign languages it may come as a surprise that not only concrete objects and actions can be named by them, but also abstract concepts and reasoning.

Project Washoe was terminated in October 1970, when Washoe herself was transferred to the Institute of Primate Studies at the University of Oklahoma in Norman. By that time she had acquired a vocabulary of 130 signs and had been observed to use 245 combinations ("phrases") of three or more of these signs.

The Gardners taught Washoe many of these signs by patient repetition. In view of the chimpanzee's known ability for imitation, this outcome is not too striking. Much more interesting was Washoe's frequently observed ability to create *new* signs and accept their use by humans in the way she had proposed. For instance, she introduced the sign "hurry" by vigorously shaking her open hand at the wrist. For "funny," she snorted and pressed her index finger against the nose. This became an accepted sign through interaction with the humans. As the Gardners explain it, the sign "first appeared as a spontaneous babble that lent itself to a simple imitation game—first Washoe signed 'funny,' then we did, then she did, and so on. We would laugh and smile during the interchanges that she initiated, and initiate the game ourselves when something funny happened. Eventually Washoe came to use the 'funny' sign spontaneously in roughly appropriate situations" [56].°

The errors committed by Washoe were at least as revealing as her successes. She was shown replicas or slides of such things as animals, foods or grooming articles and had to name them. (Great care was taken to avoid the Clever Hans phenomenon by eliminating any chance of cues from

° It should be mentioned here that the Gardners and their assistants used only ASL with Washoe and among themselves in Washoe's presence. However, nonspeech vocalizations (laughter, sounds of displeasure, etc.), as well as whistling, clapping hands, etc., were freely used.

the experimenters.) Washoe would sign "dog" for the picture of a cat, "brush" when she was shown the picture of a comb, or "food" instead of meat. All these mistakes are significant because they are not random but reveal correct conceptual grouping. The last one, "food" instead of meat, is particularly interesting as it seems to imply that a chimpanzee is capable of thinking in terms of classes of objects—an ability that for a long time was considered an exclusively human achievement and that, as we shall soon see, two other primate researchers (the Premacks) were able to prove experimentally. Similarly and for quite a long time, Washoe would often sign "baby" indiscriminately for toy cats, toy dogs, etc., but never for the real animal or its picture.

Washoe soon began to combine signs into phrases, passing from the mere naming of things (one of the most archaic ways of putting order into one's world) to communications to and about her world. Her first "phrases" were requests: "gimme sweet" and "come open." They soon became more complex, including, for instance, the name of the person to whom the request was made: "Roger you tickle." Her sign for "open" has an interesting history. Very much like a child, Washoe would at first demand the opening of a door by pounding it with the palms or knuckles of both hands. Since this is also the beginning position for the "open" sign in ASL, the Gardners taught her to complete it by drawing her hands apart and rotating the palms up. Washoe quickly transferred the use of this sign to other appropriate contexts—the refrigerator, cupboards, drawers, boxes, even briefcases and jars, and finally to faucets. This demonstrates clearly that she had not simply learned a trick, but that she must have grasped the meaning of the sign and with it the abstract concept of "opening something that is closed." Here, too, she began to use combinations of signs, and on twelve separate occasions she was observed signaling at a locked door the following phrases: *gimme key, more key, gimme key more, open key, key open, open more, more open, key in, please, open gimme key, in open help, help key in* and *open key help hurry* [48].

These examples may give the impression that Washoe strings signs together rather indiscriminately, but the Gardners report that she is quite capable of putting them in a semantically correct order. "You me go out hurry" is an example; even more impressive is her correct distinction between the meaning of "you tickle me" and "me tickle you" [50]. She also participates in what, by any definition, are dialogues. For instance:

Washoe: Out out!
Person: Who out?
Washoe: You
Person: Who more [else]?
Washoe: Me [49]

She is even capable of "talking" to herself: the Gardners observed her signing "hurry" during a speedy retreat toward her potty.

Another significant development was that Washoe's communications went beyond mere requests which, after all, are very common among animals, especially among those who live together in socially organized groups. What matters in such groups is the order of relationship between members, and as the anthropologist Gregory Bateson has pointed out repeatedly (e.g. [15]), a request for food is conveyed through behavior that invokes a certain pattern of relationship; that is, it signals "be mother to me now," rather than "I want food," as a human might put it. But when Washoe learned to signal "listen dog" at the barking of an unseen dog outside, or when she spontaneously signed "listen eat" at the sound of an alarm clock signaling mealtime, she was obviously going beyond mere naming and requests to something that might perhaps be called denotative statements (i.e., statements about the objects of her perception and, therefore, about her second-order reality).

Since her transfer to the Institute of Primate Studies at the University of Oklahoma in Norman, Washoe has made further progress. Dr. Roger Fouts, the principal investigator, reports that on one occasion she signed "gimme rock berry." This was a new combination, and apparently an incorrect one. But as it turned out, Washoe meant a box of Brazil nuts. (Similarly, Lucy, another of Fouts's chimpanzees, was for the first time given a radish, tried it, spit it out and called it "cry hurt food.") One of Washoe's funniest "remarks," also reported by Fouts, was made after a fight with a rhesus monkey. She called him "dirty monkey," although until then she had used the sign "dirty" only as a noun and in relation to feces and the like. Since then she has used it consistently as an adjective to describe people who refuse her requests [43].

Another very interesting phenomenon is the use of ASL by the Oklahoma chimpanzees among themselves. Fouts and his co-workers have observed this most frequently with tickling, play, mutual comforting and sharing. Since the chimps also continue to use their natural communications in these contexts, it does not seem exaggerated to say that they are bilingual—very much like children who grow up abroad and use both their mother tongue and the foreign language among themselves.

Since we are only at the beginning of establishing a shared reality through communication with the apes, everything reported so far raises more questions than it provides answers. We do not yet know what the upper limits of a chimp's ASL vocabulary are, and we know very little about two very important aspects of language—the use of questions and the use of negations ("not" statements) by the animals themselves. There is, however, at least some evidence from recent studies suggesting that both these concepts are within chimpanzees' reach. Fouts's chimpanzee Lucy sometimes plays with her toy cat and asks it the names of objects [44]. Of course, one may claim that Lucy is merely imitating her experimenters; that is, that she plays "experimenter" with her toy by asking "What is this? What is that?" just as *she* is being asked to name things. As far as negations are concerned, I know of two incidents in which they were observed in the communication of a three-year-old female gorilla, Koko, who is being trained in ASL at Stanford University by Penny Patterson, a graduate student. Koko signs "cannot" when she is sitting on her potty but is unable to produce. The other occurrence is a more indirect negation: when Koko is swinging and Miss Patterson points to the clock and signs "time to eat," Koko sometimes continues to swing and signs back "time to swing" [122].

Project Sarah

Probably the most sophisticated project in the area of man-chimpanzee communication is being carried out by David and Ann Premack at the University of California, Santa Barbara. Their African-born chimpanzee Sarah, who was six years old at the beginning of the study, was taught to communicate through plastic tokens with magnetized backs that could be arranged at will on a metal board. Not only has the Premack study already thrown a great deal of light on general problems of language learning, it also seems destined to put an end to many chauvinistic human presumptions about language ability in animals. Premack has published a detailed report on this work in *Science* [136].

The Premack study deals with words, sentences, questions, negations, metalinguistics (the use of language in order to teach language), class concepts (e.g., color, shape, size), verbs (the so-called copula, linking a subject with its predicate), the quantifiers *all, none, one* and *several,* and finally the important logical connective *if-then,* the basis of all thinking in terms of cause and effect.

Sarah was first trained to associate a plastic token with each word. Neither the shape nor the color of these tokens has any similarity with the object for which they stand. They are arbitrary conventions, like most words in human speech which have no immediate resemblance to what they signify. (As Bateson and Jackson once put it: "There is nothing particularly five-like in the number five; there is nothing particularly table-like in the word 'table' " [14].) To establish the association between the real object and the plastic sign chosen to stand for it, the Premacks, for instance, put a piece of fruit in front of Sarah and let her eat it. They would next place another piece of the same kind of fruit together with its sign in front of Sarah. Eventually they would put only the sign on the table and keep the fruit out of her sight. When Sarah placed the sign on the board, she was rewarded with the fruit. She learned this procedure almost immediately.

This simple method of establishing associations between a specific sign and a specific fruit was extended to cover other types of fruit, "named" by other signs, and used to teach her the names of her human companions, and eventually words other than names. In this way Sarah learned the use of verbs, arriving at sentences like "Sarah give apple Mary" when she was offered a piece of chocolate in exchange for her apple.

By patiently and consistently building up her language repertory, the Premacks have shown that a chimpanzee is capable of such "human" mental operations as the use of questions, negations, the comparisons *same* and *different,* the metalinguistic concept *name of* and *not name of* (as, for instance, in the question "? name of dish," meaning "What is the name of this dish?," or "? 'banana' name of apple," meaning "Is the sign 'banana' the name of the object apple?" and requiring the correct answer through the use of the "yes" or "no" sign). But to me the most surprising result of this study is the fact that the chimpanzee can order her universe into logical classes. Sarah correctly assigns a watermelon to either the class of fruit, the class of food or the class of round objects, depending on the nature of the question put to her. This means that all the problems we encounter in clinical work with humans that arise out of the paradox-engendering confusion of a class with a member of that class are at least potentially present also in the apes. One is left wondering if logicians and philosophers, from the ancient Greeks to Whitehead and Russell, ever dreamed of this possibility!

Of necessity, the treatment here of the area of man-animal communication is extremely sketchy and cannot, for lack of space, mention all the work that is going on—for instance, Rumbough, Gill and von Glaserfeld's computer-trained chimpanzee Lana [147]. But I hope I have shown that whatever the limits of communication between man and the apes may turn out to be, our human chauvinism has been severely shaken by the undeniable fact that they and not we were the first organisms to learn the language of another species.

Yet another important consideration follows from these studies. The natural environment of apes is such that they are hardly ever called upon to perform the remarkable achievements of which we now know them to be capable. In other words, their mental abilities are potentially far greater than their everyday life in the wild seems to require, but they can be brought out and developed in completely "unnatural" contacts with humans. This raises precisely the same question with regard to ourselves: How much of our own potential are we actually using and what superhuman trainers could help us to develop it further?

16

The Dolphin

I have come across a story which is true although it sounds very much like a fable, and is worthy of your exuberant, elevated and truly poetic genius. I heard it the other day over supper, when miraculous events of all kinds were discussed. The man who told it is fully trustworthy. But what does trustworthiness matter to a poet? However, you could rely on this man even if you were writing history.

There is in Africa a Roman settlement, called Hippo, located near the sea. It lies on the shore of a navigable lagoon; from this a river-like estuary opens into the sea and, depending on the tides, its waters are carried into the sea or pushed into the lagoon. Here people of all ages like to fish, sail and also swim, especially the boys, who love to play here. Their glory is to be carried out to sea: and he who leaves the shore and his companions farthest behind is the winner. In one of these contests a boy who was bolder than the others was getting far out. A dolphin appeared and first swam in front of him, then followed him, then played around him, lifted him up and rolled him down, took him on his back again and carried the frightened lad out to sea. But then it turned back towards the shore and restored him to the dry land and his companions.

The news of this event spread quickly through the settlement: everybody came running to see the boy, as if there were something miraculous about him, and they questioned him, listened to his account and passed it around. [130]

This letter of Pliny the Younger, written around A.D. 98 to his poet friend Caninius, reflects the strange fascination that dolphins, those fabulous creatures from the open seas, have exerted over humans for millennia.

This fascination is difficult to define. There is something about the dolphin° that appeals to the human mind more and differently than the charm of any other animal. Pliny's remark that people flocked around the boy as if he were a kind of prodigy is probably not exaggerated. Most people who have observed or worked with the dolphin agree that there is something very unusual about his influence on humans. There is one story in particular, told by Antony Alpers in his delightful book on dolphins [6], that reads like a modern version of Pliny's letter:

In 1955 the inhabitants of the small town of Opononi on the north island of New Zealand became aware of a young female dolphin who almost daily came into their harbor and began to follow boats and swimmers. Eventually she befriended some children and allowed herself to be

° Since most of what follows in this section is about the bottle-nosed dolphin *(Tursiops truncatus)*, I shall use the term dolphin rather than porpoise. Together with the whales (which share many of their characteristics), both dolphins and porpoises belong to the order *Cetacea*.

touched. She seemed to be particularly fond of a thirteen-year-old girl whom she would occasionally pick up and carry on her back for short distances. And just as at Hippo eighteen centuries before, the story of the dolphin spread rapidly, and people came from near and far to see her. Soon there were thousands of people jamming the village, clogging the coastal road and camping on the beach. The dolphin, nicknamed Opo, seemed to enjoy their presence and never failed to show up. But what was most remarkable was that, to use Alpers' words, "on this mass of sunburned, jostling humanity, the gentle dolphin had the effect of a benediction." The villagers noticed that unlike other years, there were no fights, arguments or drunkenness. "Some people got so excited when they saw Opo," wrote one of the villagers, "that they went into the water fully clothed, just to touch her."

In the evenings, when it was too chilly to be in the water any longer and the dolphin had gone off, everyone talked about her. In the tents that glowed like pale green lanterns under the pine-trees, the campers exchanged their scanty knowledge of the marvel, speaking in low voices while the children slept. They visited each other's tents, becoming friends with total strangers in an instant, all because of the dolphin. And in the hotel dining-room, everyone talked to everyone. There was such an overflow of these friendly feelings that it seemed the crowds were composed of people wanting to be forgiven for something—for the unkindness, perhaps, that humans generally do to animals in the wild. The dolphin, who never once snapped at a hand, seemed to offer forgiveness for all. [7]

Even the hard scientific data about the dolphin are remarkable. There is, first of all, the fact of their enormous brains, and here is some basic information which is indispensable for our subsequent considerations:

The size of an organism's brain has both absolute and relative importance. The larger and therefore more complex the brain, the more complex and sophisticated its functioning. These increases are not continuous, however; the emergence of new and higher functions occurs in a stepwise fashion. For instance, there is a critical limit: at around 1,000 grams the richness of a brain's organization (interconnectivity) enables the organism to use symbols and therefore permits the development of language.° (With an average brain weight of 375 grams, the adult chimpanzee is well below this limit, which may account for its inability to develop any kind of language spontaneously.) The adult human brain has an average weight of 1,450 grams, the brain of the big whales is six times and that of the elephant four times heavier than ours. However, in both the whale and the elephant the *relative* size of the brain (the ratio of brain weight to body weight) is well below that of the human brain. On the other hand the dolphin, one of the smaller whales, not only has a brain whose absolute weight (about 1,700 grams) is above that of the human but has a body of approximately comparable size.

Granting that millions of years ago the dolphin returned to the sea *after* adapting to life on land, which scientists believe to be the case, the question as to why this creature is equipped with such a superbrain still remains unanswered. One may speculate that had dolphins remained on land, they might have developed into a species superior to us. But they returned to the sea and thus had to forgo certain developments which, in absence of evidence to the con-

---

° This provides a good example of a general law of systems, namely, that increases in their complexity bring about stepwise, discontinuous increments of their functioning. These increases are virtually impossible to predict. We shall briefly return to this phenomenon on pages 203 ff., when discussing the possible complexity of extraterrestrial civilizations.

trary, we must consider crucial for the emergence of a civilized race. Dolphin hands turned into flippers (as evidenced by the fact that their skeletal structure is still that of a hand), and without hands there can be no invention and use of tools, no direct influence over the environment, no development of writing, and therefore no information storage and tradition.

Of course, dolphins had no need to develop in this direction; they live in the weightlessness provided by the buoyancy of water, they do not have to construct shelters or find clothing, and food is usually plentiful, so there is no reason to learn how to grow and store it. Except for man, they have few natural enemies, principally sharks and killer whales, and they are adept at defending themselves against the former and escaping the latter. What then, do they do with their brains? It takes very little intelligence to live in the sea. The whale shark, for instance, has survived for millions of years with a brain the size of a monkey's in a body weighing up to forty tons.

Not surprisingly, dolphins are the object of intense scientific interest. It simply does not make sense to assume that all they can do with their excess intelligence is jump over the bow waves of ships, perform useless, undignified tricks in amusement parks, or help the Navy blow up enemy ships. Furthermore, of all the animals with superior brains, only dolphins are a manageable research object for humans; the purely technical problems of working with big whales or with elephants are overwhelming.

Since dolphins are lung breathers, they have to come to the surface for air and are therefore as much in danger of drowning as we humans. (In fact, it is estimated that about a hundred thousand of them drown every year after getting entangled in fishing nets.) This accounts for the astonishing and touching helpfulness they show not only among themselves but also toward humans who are in trouble in the sea.

There are numerous contemporary eyewitness reports confirming what Aristotle, Plutarch and Pliny observed many centuries ago—that dolphins rescue both their own kind and drowning humans by lifting the bodies to the surface. They continue to do this for many hours, constantly taking turns. Thanks to detailed studies by means of hydrophones (underwater microphones), we now know that a disabled dolphin emits what we might be tempted to call an international emergency signal, which immediately brings others to its aid. This signal° can be imitated by humans, and I know of a young zoology student who tried it: he dove to the bottom of the dolphin tank and emitted the distress call. Immediately the two dolphins lifted him bodily to the surface. What happened then is of the greatest interest to the communication researcher and the social scientist alike. The dolphins observed that he was all right and apparently realized at once that he had misused the distress signal. They gave him what in human terms would amount to a sound thrashing, pummeling him with their bony snouts and slapping him with their tails. Different as their world may be from ours, here is a rule that holds in both: the misuse of a vital signal is serious misbehavior which, in the interest of all concerned, cannot be tolerated. Under just about any other known circumstances, the dolphin's friendliness toward human beings is proverbial, even under severe provocation or threat.

Especially in captivity the dolphins' awareness of human behavior and human limitations is surprising. For instance, they seem to be aware of a human's proficiency in swimming. Captive dolphins have been observed pushing swimmers to the side of the tank and trying to lift them out of it. This has been interpreted to mean that they consid-

° Lilly describes it as "a very short, sharp, high-pitched whistle, in two parts, a crescendo and a decrescendo in pitch" [88].

ered the human's swimming ability insufficient for him to be in the deep tank, although, of course, they may have wanted him out for quite different reasons. (However, I am proud to say that when I went into the same tank, my ability to swim underwater seemed to impress the dolphins favorably; they made no attempt to rescue me and very soon started to propose various games.) The dolphins' vocalizations (of which more will be said later) are usually well above the frequency audible to the human ear. Quite amazingly, captive dolphins soon become aware of this and lower their frequency to levels that we can perceive. They also discover that we cannot hear them under water (except, of course, by hydrophones) and therefore lift their blowholes out of the water when they want to be heard.

I just mentioned games. While it is true that young dolphins in particular are naturally playful and that highly complex forms of game behavior have been observed, many investigators believe that there is an interesting problem of punctuation involved here. It is not so much that dolphins happen to be organisms that can do tricks (as their amusement-park performances would seem to indicate), but rather that they have discovered that *we* can be taught to do tricks. Forrest Wood of the Marine Studios in Florida reports:

> All of the younger animals that were born in the tank have become adept at this. They have found that if they toss the rubber ring to someone standing at the rail, that person will quickly learn to throw it back, and will continue the game until the porpoise tires of it. That two creatures of such unlike habit and habitat have learned to share an activity that yields mutual enjoyment speaks well, I think, for both porpoise and man. [188]

This leads to another impression that almost inevitably

imposes itself: dolphins appear anxious to establish communication with us and seem pleased when they succeed. Perhaps it would be more correct to say that they grow impatient if they fail. Or perhaps this entire impression is read into their behavior by the human observer who finds it only too easy to be carried away into wild anthropomorphizing by the beauty and seductive charms of these creatures. (This ever-present danger, by the way, has also been known to work the other way around; animals zoomorphize—that is, see us in terms of their reality.)

This brings us back to the heart of our subject—the establishment of communication with nonhuman intelligence. Here is an organism with an intelligence equal (maybe superior) to ours, inhabiting a totally different world (the sea), apparently as deeply interested in us as we are in it and desirous to enter into communication with us. What, then, are the possibilities?

The answer, I am afraid, is disappointingly anticlimactic. In spite of an enormous amount of work by many researchers, the code of their intraspecies communication has not been broken. There is no doubt that dolphins communicate in highly complex ways among themselves but—and this may seem a flat contradiction—the experts are in disagreement over the question of whether there is really a dolphin "language." To be sure, even in absence of a natural dolphin language, an artificial language could be devised that both human and dolphin could share. There are two avenues of approach.

One would be to use human speech as the basic vehicle. This would be very much the equivalent of the early attempts to teach our language to chimpanzees. Imitations of human speech by dolphins in captivity have been observed and recorded; the interested reader is referred to a taped lecture by Dr. John Lilly, the former director of the Communications Research Laboratory at Nazareth Bay, St.

Thomas, in the Virgin Islands [91], which contains the recording of what Lilly claims are the words "All right, let's go!" uttered at the beginning of a training session by one of the dolphins after the experimenter had said them in a loud voice. Apart from the fact that this feat could also be accomplished by a parrot or a mynah bird, the trouble with these funny squeals is that unless the listener is told their supposed meaning before actually hearing them, he is not able to identify them and would be just as likely to agree that the dolphin said, "I swear, it's cold," if told that *that* was their meaning.° The organ of the dolphin's vocalizations, the blowhole, seems to be even less suited to the production of human speech than the chimpanzee's voice box.

The other possibility would be to base man-dolphin communication on a system congenial to the dolphin's natural vocalizations. To make them audible to the human ear, these signals would have to be brought down to a frequency within the human range.† This presents no technical problems, but it would slow down the signals by a factor of about eight. Consequently, even a few seconds after the beginning of a test, the observers would be hopelessly behind in time, and it would become virtually impossible to relate a certain behavior to the vocalization that accompanied it, except by sophisticated underwater

° Lilly is aware of this possible source of error. In an earlier publication he reports that one evening somebody in the laboratory said very loudly, "It's six o'clock." One of the dolphins in the tank then produced a sound which some observers thought was a poor imitation of this sentence. But to Lilly it sounded more like "This is a trick," said with a peculiar hissing accent. Several others of his colleagues who heard the tape came to the same conclusion [88].

† Human speech covers a frequency range of 100–5,000 cycles per second; dolphins use 3,000–20,000 c/sec, and occasionally even frequencies up to 120,000 cycles are observed.

filming of the entire behavior and studying the film at the same slow speed as the sound recording.

It must also be borne in mind that a very large part of the dolphins' acoustic emissions are not communications of the kind we have so far considered in this book, but rather part of their extremely sophisticated system of echolocation. The reader is probably aware that bats are capable of flying in darkness by emitting shrill sounds (usually well above human hearing) that bounce back from the obstacles in their path and thus enable the bats to avoid them. Sonar and radar systems utilize this principle for navigation and in astronomy. For the dolphins it constitutes their most important sensory modality. It is their communication system with the world around them, except that its code is one-sided—it is both question and answer. Water is an excellent sound conductor, and as the dolphins move through it they emit high-frequency signals, which are reflected from the objects around them and supply three types of data:

1. The location of the object and, therefore, also the direction and speed of any movement of this object;
2. its distance;
3. its size, shape and texture.

In other words, thanks to these high-frequency echoes (the "answers") of the signals produced by the dolphins (the "questions"), they constantly reconstruct in their brain a very accurate picture of their surroundings. To achieve this they evidently utilize the delay with which the signals reach their right and left ears, respectively, to compute the object's location (very much as we identify the location of a source of sound); they use the delay between the emission of a signal and the return of its echo as a reliable indication of its distance; and finally, they seem to possess a vast amount of information about the typical distortions of the echo, permitting them to identify the nature, texture, hardness and other properties of the sound-reflecting object. This latter ability enables dolphins not only to fish in darkness or in murky water but also to identify different kinds of fish—presumably being fully aware of what a given type of fish "looks" like acoustically. Indeed, there seems to be reason to assume that the dolphins' sonar system is so efficient that it provides a kind of acoustic "X-ray vision"— that is, information that goes beyond the surface of the reflecting objects. There is some evidence that dolphin mothers are aware of a coliclike distress in their young, presumably because the infants' sonar reflection is significantly changed as a result of the bloating, and they have been observed gently tapping their infants' bellies to make them burp, just as a human mother would.

All this tells us that dolphins live in a predominantly acoustic world, while our picture of reality is mostly visual. This complicates the establishment of a shared reality, especially since it has not yet been established how dolphins communicate among themselves—we know only that they have the one-sided echolocation code.

On the other hand, it would be difficult to overlook the great mass of circumstantial evidence that the dolphins' communication goes beyond the mere warning and distress calls and other emotive signals that exist almost universally among members of the same species. One of the most impressive examples of this is reported by R. B. Robinson, the author of *On Whales and Men*, and involves the dolphin's larger relative, the killer whale. According to this report, a fishing fleet operating in the Antarctic was harassed by the invasion of thousands of killer whales, feasting on the fish near the boats. The fishing fleet called for help from a nearby whaling fleet. Both fleets were using the same type of boats, converted Navy corvettes with identical hulls and the same type of engine. One of the whaling boats fired a single shot from its harpoon gun and killed a whale. Within half an hour the whales had completely disappeared from an area of some fifty square miles around the whaling boats that had been sent to the help of the fishing fleet, while in other areas they continued to interfere with the fishing [144].

The conclusions to be drawn from this story are far-reaching. For the whales, the only difference between the two types of vessels was that the whaling boats prominently displayed the harpoon guns on their prows. Since they withdrew from the gun boats but remained around the fishing boats, the dying whale must have communicated this crucial piece of information. This is far more sophisticated than the usual warning signals of animals. The whale's message *must* have contained detailed, factual, denotative information—a feat that was, and still generally is, considered an exclusively human achievement. It is one thing to express an emotion, such as fear, in a way that alerts other members of the same species to an immediate danger; it is quite another thing to specify the physical appearance of the dangerous object and its effect. To achieve this the organism needs more than the simple expression of emotions; it needs something identical to human language. To rephrase this in more practical terms: to scream "Ouch!" is one thing; to shout "Get your big foot off my toes!" is a very different type of communication.

If this incident with the killer whales took place exactly as reported by Robinson, it would greatly strengthen the assumption that whales, and presumably dolphins as well, are indeed of superior intelligence and do have a language. But we are again faced with the question of what they do with this intelligence. As I said earlier, we do not know. It may well be that we are in for a disappointment and that while the dolphins' intelligence is undoubtedly great, their behavior in captivity at best resembles that of a human hebephrenic with their cryptic but empty innuendos and their clowning without humor. If this is the case, we still have to ask ourselves, What have we done to these gentle creatures from the sea?

What we have done so far, by and large, is to teach them tricks. And whether the locale is an amusement park or a research institute, dolphins have shown themselves to be as eager trainees as they are willing subjects for research. They are being studied by scientists all over the world (for instance, at the universities of Cambridge, Hawaii, Berne, Berlin, Adelaide and Moscow), but unfortunately partially for quite sinister reasons. That physicists should be interested in the astonishing fact that dolphins can sustain speeds of 25 miles per hour, which is about ten times more than they "should" achieve with the muscle power available to them, is understandable.° But it is rumored—and for very obvious reasons no evidence to support these rumors is available—that the military have been experimenting with whales and dolphins for less harmless activities than retrieving practice torpedoes from the ocean floor. There are persistent stories about training them to track submarines or to attach explosive charges to the hulls of ships or to underwater military installations. A certain harbor in South Vietnam is believed to have been successfully protected against frogmen by dolphins that had been trained to kill. If

° Experiments with dead dolphins have shown that to move their bodies through the water at a speed of 15 kilometers per hour (a speed easily achieved and maintained by the dolphins) requires a force of 1.25 kilowatts, which is about seven times as much as the dolphins can muster. Scientists now believe that the dolphins' smooth skin somehow manages to minimize the surface drag that creates most of the resistance experienced by man and man-made craft. There is also now photographic evidence that when accelerating and when swimming at high speeds, dolphins develop certain skin corrugations on their sides which are believed to account for their seemingly effortless speed. Their tail propulsion is superior in output to that of propellors, and the principle may eventually be adapted to the propulsion of ships.

this is true, we humans are entitled to the sad claim of having managed to terminate three thousand years of recorded history, attesting to the dolphins' gentle and helpful nature in their relations to man, and to have taught these patient creatures to become murderers.

Fortunately, world-wide demand for the protection of whales and dolphins is growing, especially since some whales are in danger of becoming extinct. Lilly reports that as far as the dolphins are concerned, the USSR has taken the initiative: in March 1966, the Soviet Ministry of Fisheries issued a decree prohibiting the commercial catching and slaughter of dolphins in the Black Sea and the Sea of Azov for a period of ten years. Several members of the Soviet Academy of Sciences have appealed to their colleagues all over the world to achieve similar bans in their countries [90].

Lilly himself has been very outspoken in his demand for the legal protection of the cetaceans. He believes that because of the high level of their development, we should consider them our equals. Speaking specifically of the sperm whale with its enormous brain, he suggests that instead of killing it, we should make the utmost effort to acquaint it with the level of our own achievement. To give the reader a taste of Lilly's sometimes exuberant ideas, here is a quotation from one of his books:

> Probably that which would excite the most respect for the human species in a sperm whale would be a full symphony orchestra playing a symphony. At least this would be an excellent starter to try to convince a sperm whale that maybe some of us are better than just in-concert murderers of whales. A symphony orchestra playing multiple melodies and their complex transformations might keep him interested for at least two or three hours. With his huge computer the sperm whale could probably store the whole symphony

and play it back in his mind to himself at his leisure. I suggest that whoever tries this experiment first should be ready to play several symphonies, each symphony only once. Otherwise the sperm whale would be bored with the performance. [89]

Whether this particular experiment is feasible or not, the mere thought that there are living beings on our planet whose intelligence approaches if it does not surpass ours, who share our world and yet live in a totally different reality, is so enormously intriguing that we shall never cease to wonder what they know and what their reality is like.

It probably did not come as a surprise to Dr. Lilly when, in 1961, he received an invitation to attend a meeting sponsored by the U.S. National Academy of Sciences. The meeting was organized for a select group of astronomers and astrophysicists who presumably knew very little of dolphins and whales but had no difficulty realizing the importance and relevance of Lilly's work for their own projects. In fact, so impressed were they by his presentation that they decided to form the Order of the Dolphins, an expression of the *esprit de corps* of a small group of scientists dedicated to the same goal: the establishment of communication with nonhuman intelligence. Lilly was searching for it in the ocean; they were looking for it in outer space.

17

Extraterrestrial Communication

Is there intelligent life beyond our planet? As far as our own solar system is concerned, the answer has been a clear *no* even before the advent of space flights. Even if life should eventually be found on Mars or another planet, it would be of a very rudimentary nature (amino acids, bacteria, perhaps lichens), but nothing even remotely approaching little green men in unidentified flying objects.

If we extend our question beyond the solar system, the answer is almost certainly *yes*. To understand why this is so we must place our question in perspective, and the perspective is truly cosmic:

First of all, astrophysical laymen find it hard to believe that if intelligent life were found within our galaxy (the Milky Way), its forms would have to be very similar to life on earth. This is because there is solid evidence that the Milky Way is composed largely of the same four basic elements that make up 99 percent of our terrestrial matter: carbon, hydrogen, nitrogen and oxygen. This makes it most unlikely that totally different organisms could have evolved on other planets—for instance, beings that could exist in a temperature of bubbling lava or the icy, airless climate of some distant cousin of our moon. Learn your biochemistry here on earth, Nobel Prize-winner Professor George Wald likes to tell his students, and you will be able to pass your examinations on Arcturus.

Our question is now narrowed down to this: How many planets are there in our galaxy whose age, distance from their own sun, and other general physical conditions, such as an atmosphere with a temperature in the life-sustaining heat zone, are comparable to ours? Although modern estimates vary considerably, Sir Arthur Eddington's rule of thumb is still generally accepted: 10^{11} stars make up a galaxy, and 10^{11} galaxies make the universe.° On the strength of cogent reasoning, which we shall here accept on faith, 1 to 5 percent of these stars (suns) may be surrounded by several planets offering life-sustaining conditions. And now we have our answer: a billion planets in our Milky Way could harbor life similar to or even much more evolved than our own. The wish to enter into communication with these organisms is, therefore, no science-fiction pipe dream but a very legitimate and, indeed, urgent scientific task.

This does not, of course, mean that these planets actually have life on them. It only means that they *may*. Our biologists know far too little about the development of life on earth to draw reliable conclusions about its appearance and presence in outer space. It may turn out to be a

° Ten to the eleventh power, it will be remembered, is the number 1 followed by eleven zeros—an unimaginable magnitude.

common, almost inevitable outcome once certain fundamental conditions are met, or it may be, very much in Jacques Monod's sense, the outcome of a fantastically small chance [102].

However, as the cosmologist Martin Rees said, "absence of evidence is not evidence of absence," and the only scientific attitude to take in the face of this uncertainty is to assume that intelligent life does exist in and beyond our galaxy. Once we have accepted this, the question of establishing communication demands an answer.

Actually there are two questions involved. The first concerns the strictly technical aspects of communication over such enormous distances, the *how*, so to speak. Intimately connected with this is the second question, the *what*, namely the complex problem of offering to these alien creatures, with their totally unknown ways of thinking, speaking and of punctuating their second-order reality, certain understandable proposals for communication with, and disclosures about, ourselves.

The difference between the *how* and the *what* requires further explanation. Suppose that two people, each equipped with a radio transmitter and receiver, want to establish communication. They cannot do this unless they have agreed *beforehand* on such basic technicalities as frequency (wave length), code, call signals, transmission times, etc. Without first agreeing on these procedural matters (the *how* of their wireless traffic), the chances they would have for entering into communication would be virtually zero. Notice, however, that the *what* presents no problems and need not be coordinated beforehand: they understand the language in which the messages are sent (if necessary with the help of a translator), and both being humans living in the same physical universe at the same time and sharing a virtually immeasurable amount of information about their human condition and their environment, they will have no need to work out a basis of common understanding. In the case of extraterrestrial communication, both the *how* and the *what* have to be found and established.

In science fiction the problem of how extraterrestrial communication can be established is neatly solved by the use of powerful spaceships traveling to the remotest reaches of space with the speed of light. Outside of science fiction, only one thing is known for sure: if we do get in contact with civilizations on other planets, it will *not* be by means of manned spaceships. First of all, the distances involved are enormous. If our entire solar system were contained in a room of a house in San Francisco, the nearest star would be in Tokyo. But there is no guarantee that this star would happen to be orbited by one of the billion habitable planets, and in order to have a statistically fair chance of coming upon one of these planets one would have to travel about 200 times farther out into space. Even if we someday manage to build a spacecraft that travels as fast as physically possible, namely close to the speed of light, no human being could get there and back within his lifetime— even though there is reason to believe that biological aging would be much slower under these circumstances.° And as

° This is not science fiction, but a cogent deduction from the theory of relativity. One of the more unimaginable properties of the reality postulated by relativity theory is that time itself is not absolute, and that a lengthening, a dilation, of time will occur in any system approaching the speed of light. This means that astronauts traveling at such speeds would eventually return to earth to find that everything down here had aged much more than they. Von Hoerner computed the time on earth and the time experienced by the crew of a spaceship and found that as the length of an interplanetary voyage increases, the difference rises steeply (exponentially). Two years for the crew would only be slightly longer on earth, namely 2.1 years, but ten crew years would be 24 earth years, and the astronomer Frank Drake pointed out in a recent talk, another problem would be that the spaceship would have to have the weight of about a thousand battleships and would burn up half of the earth's atmosphere on takeoff.

Radio communication is a very different matter. Quoting Drake again, for ten cents' worth of electricity one can send a ten-word telegram 100 light-years into space.° Quite obviously, then, this is the most feasible form of communication. Astrophysicists have at their disposal radio telescopes, built specifically for deep-space exploration, which can be used for precisely the purpose we are now considering. One of the most powerful instruments in existence is Cornell University's radio telescope at Arecibo in Puerto Rico. Its range is so vast that it could detect the pulses originating from an identical instrument anywhere in our galaxy. In other words, if another civilization, existing in even the remotest distance of the Milky Way, had reached our level of technical progress, radio communication between them and us would be technically possible by means of the instruments that we already possess.†

But this is not the whole story. There is another, unplanned and unintended way in which other civilizations

---

thirty astronaut years would be 3,100 terrestrial years. Doubling the crew years to sixty would amount to 5 million years on our planet [71].

° One light-year (i.e., the distance light travels in a solar year) is about 5.87 million million miles.

† An even larger radio telescope, sponsored by the National Science Foundation, is under construction in an ancient lake bed on the eastern slopes of the Continental Divide in New Mexico. It should be completed in 1981 and will consist of twenty-seven parabolic disk antennas, each almost 30 meters in diameter.

But even this would be dwarfed if Project Cyclops [137] were ever built. This would be an array of some 1,400 giant radio disk antennas, clustered together in a circular area with a diameter of approximately 16 kilometers and moving in unison. The cost of this instrument is estimated at $5 billion.

can become aware of our existence. During the last thirty years or so, our planet has increasingly become a source of man-made electromagnetic pollution in the form of ever more powerful radio and television signals, especially via space relay satellites. Our earth is now surrounded by a sphere of electronic radiation expanding at the speed of light and already reaching some 30 light-years into space. Most of the signals are weak, it is true, but they can be picked up and amplified, and their nature is such that any extraterrestrial beings advanced enough to possess the necessary receiving equipment would have no difficulty in realizing that these signals are artificial and not merely the result of natural, random radio emission.° Thirty light-years is admittedly a rather short distance even within our own galaxy, but if we continue to send out television broadcasts (rather than, say, switch to cable TV) for another hundred years, we will be detectable over a distance of more than 100 light-years, and this means roughly 1,000 stellar systems, every one of which may have one or more life-sustaining planets.

Whether communication with other civilizations in space will eventually be established actively through special messages sent out or received for this very purpose, or passively through the detection of radio and television signals, the important thing will be the acquisition—that is, the detection of our signals by others or vice versa. At the present state of the art, acquisition would be an unbeliev-

---

° Professor I. S. Shklovsky of the Soviet Academy of Sciences points out that through the development of television alone, our planet is now second in "brightness temperature" (i.e., of radio emissions) only to the sun in our solar system [164]. This could be embarrassing, for, bearing in mind the rubbish that our news media put out, it is quite possible that extraterrestrial civilizations may have an all too realistic picture of us long before we get a chance to impress them with what *we* think they should know about us.

ably lucky chance event. We have the necessary transmitting and receiving equipment (the radio telescopes), but no direct way of establishing the most essential preconditions for successful radio communication: frequencies and times. We do not even know if there is anybody out there, and if so, where. Astronomers have good reason to favor certain areas of our galaxy rather than others for this purpose, but even so, the chances of having a terrestrial radio telescope listening or transmitting in the right direction on the right frequency at the right time are very small. From a communications point of view, the frequency problem is the most interesting.

The problem is paradoxical. An agreement on frequency presupposes communication, but communication is exactly what we want to establish by using the right frequency. How can we arrive at the right decision in absence of communication? At this point we return to the question of interdependence and of *what* the basis of our communication with extraterrestrials can be.

Anticryptography

The idea of communication with extraterrestrial beings turned from science fiction into science in 1959 with the publication by Giuseppe Cocconi and Philip Morrison, both of Cornell University, of a brief paper entitled "Searching for Interstellar Communications" [33]. At what frequency shall we look, they asked and then answered:

A long spectrum search for a weak signal of unknown frequency is difficult. But, just in the most favoured radio region there is a *unique, objective standard of frequency, which must be known to every observer in the universe:* the outstanding radio emission line at 1,420 mc /s ($\lambda = 21$ cm) of neutral hydrogen. (Italics mine.)

The italicized part of this quotation is of great significance to our subject. The reader will recall that in interdependent decision making in the absence of prior communication, a positive outcome is possible only when it is based on some tacitly shared assumption or on some element that through its obviousness—its physical prominence or some other unique quality—stands out among the numerous other possibilities. It must have been clear immediately to Cocconi and Morrison that the frequency chosen for the purpose of establishing interstellar communication had to be unique in "being known to every observer in the universe." Their reasoning is based on the same old principle "What do I know that he knows that I know . . . ?"

Long before the advent of radio astronomy and space travel, the practical problems of establishing extraterrestrial communication fascinated dreamers as well as scientists. Perhaps the most important historic example is the plan proposed by the famous mathematician Carl Friedrich Gauss in 1820. In those days optical telescopes offered the only known way of observing the skies, and any plan for space communication had to be based on visual observation. Gauss suggested that one way of making the inhabitants of other planets aware of the existence of intelligent life on earth would be to lay out a gigantic Pythagorean triangle in the Siberian forests. The lines were to be represented by 10-mile-wide strips of forest; the triangle itself and the three squares erected on its sides were to be wheat fields. In summer the yellow wheat would contrast with the green of the forest; in winter the contrast would be provided by the white of the snow-covered fields against the darkness of the trees. Gauss argued that the triangle would be large enough to be visible even from the more remote planets in our solar system with telescopes of the same power as the ones then existing on earth, and that the meaning of the diagram would be as obvious to extraterrestrial astronomers and mathematicians as to ourselves.° His first assumption may have been right, but it is not equally plausible that alien scientists would necessarily understand our representation of a mathematical square through the analogy of a physical one. John Macvey, on the other hand, argues convincingly that "the square of a number when translated into dimensional physical units gives a physical square so long as the lines are at right angles to one another. This fundamental truth must surely apply on *any* planet *any*where" [95]. Whether this be so or not, it is a minor point compared to the sheer magnitude of the project. Maxwell Cade took the trouble of computing the necessary area and found that it would cover 4.352 million acres of forest and 12.8 million acres of wheatfields [28].

Two other nineteenth-century proposals were even more impracticable. One was proposed by Charles Cros, a French poet and scientist,† in his book *Etude sur les moyens de communication avec les planètes* (A Study of the Means of Communication with the Planets). Among other things he suggested sending optical signals from earth to the other planets by means of powerful electric lights intensified by

---

° I have been unable to trace Gauss's idea in his prolific writings, especially since he may have mentioned it merely as an aside in one of his letters. I believe that the exact reference, as well as the bibliographical information on Littrow's project (to be mentioned presently) is contained in two Soviet publications (see references 123 and 148). I was unable to obtain this material and am presenting it here in the way it crops up repeatedly (but without an indication of the exact sources) in the literature on extraterrestrial communication.

† He lived from 1842 until 1888 and his genius, coupled with his wide range of talents and interests, made him a kind of nineteenth-century Jean Cocteau. He invented color photography, proposed the phonograph in a letter to the French Academy of Science before Edison invented it, and suggested and created art forms that made him the precursor of surrealism.

reflectors. Another of his ideas, for which he repeatedly sought funds from the French government, was to construct a huge mirror by which sunlight could be focused on Mars to melt the sand supposed to cover that planet and thus tattoo enormous inscriptions into the Martian surface. He seemed unable to appreciate—and others were obviously unable to convince him—that the sunlight beamed at Mars would always be less intense than that falling on its surface directly from the sun. His main hope appears to have been that these light signals would eventually be answered from other planets, and as he envisions this moment his style becomes lyrical:

> The observers, armed with the most powerful instruments, never cease to look at the interrogated star. And there, on the dark portion of its disc, a small luminous point appears. This is the answer! Through its intermittent flashes that repeat the terrestrial signals, this luminous point seems to say: "We have seen you; we have understood you."
>
> This will be a moment of joy and of pride for mankind. The eternal isolation of the spheres is vanquished. There is no longer a limit to the avid human curiosity [which] already restlessly ranged the Earth like a tiger his all too narrow cage. [35]

The other scheme was quite seriously proposed by the director of the Vienna observatory, Joseph Johann von Littrow, in 1840. He suggested digging a circular ditch about 20 miles in diameter in the Sahara, filling it with water and pouring kerosene on the water. This was to be lighted at night and allowed to burn for several hours. By changing the circle to squares, triangles, etc., on subsequent nights, unmistakable proof of intelligent activity would be visible far into our solar system. It did not seem to discourage von Littrow that water is a rare commodity in the desert and that the requisite quantity of kerosene would indeed be astronomical.°

Impractical as these projects were, they were all based on the fundamental realization that whatever we offer our partners in space must be something we have reason to believe is as much part of their reality as of our own. Gauss was undoubtedly right in assuming that an alien race capable of building a telescope *had* to have discovered the abstract truth of the Pythagorean theorem. How else would they have been able to put together such a sophisticated device, requiring extensive knowledge of physics, optics, mechanics and, therefore, of mathematics? Gauss's reasoning has remained the basis of all further refinements and modernizations in the planning of extraterrestrial communication. It amounts to this: the kind of code used must be the exact opposite of what a code is normally designed for— namely to ensure greatest secrecy and to make it impossible for an outsider to decipher the encoded message. Cryptography, the science of constructing and breaking codes, is another facet of the art of creating disinformation, of hiding the order inherent in all communication, and in its code-breaking aspects yet another search for order in apparent randomness.†

Research into the most useful code for interstellar messages has most appropriately been called anticryptography—that is, the art of encoding the message in so obvious and transparent a way that its decoding presents as few problems as possible and leaves the least room for error and ambiguity. As mentioned, it has to be based on those aspects of our reality that are most likely to be part of the other

---

° To quote Cade [28] again, the project would have required hundreds of thousands of tons of kerosene per night.

† The interested reader is referred to Kahn's extensive treatment of this fascinating subject [77].

race's reality. Some of these aspects are: the basic physical and chemical laws that we know hold for the entire universe, the laws of logic and mathematics (for instance, the properties of prime numbers), and particularly the fact that both we and they have developed at least one identical (or very similar) instrument, the radio telescope. Its identical functioning on both planets leads to the inescapable conclusion that both civilizations possess a considerable amount of comparable information. We may conceive of them and of ourselves as being in the same situation as those two imaginary secret agents (page 104) who must meet but do not yet know when and where to meet and must try to decide correctly what solution is the most obvious for both of them. In the case of our extraterrestrial partners, we can safely assume that they will think along very much the same lines and try to make their messages as obvious and clear to us as we try to make ours to them. Alien as those races and their second-order reality may be, we do share a great deal of first-order reality with them, and these shared aspects will obviously provide the first bridge of mutual understanding.

Let us look very briefly at what has already been done.

Project Ozma

"At approximately 4 A.M. on April 8, 1960, our world entered a new age without knowing it." With these words Macvey [94] describes a truly historic moment: mankind's first attempt to establish communication with intelligent life outside our planet. This project was called Ozma after the charming queen who ruled the distant land of Oz and its strange inhabitants.

Project Ozma was organized by the astronomer Frank

Drake at the National Radio Astronomy Observatory in Green Bank, West Virginia. Drake appreciated the cogency of Cocconi and Morrison's logic regarding the 21-cm frequency. Out of the many stars that for one astronomical reason or another appeared to be the most "eligible," Drake and his colleagues selected two, Epsilon Eridani and Tau Ceti, both approximately eleven light-years from earth, as their most likely targets. For three months these two stars were tracked alternatively by the Green Bank radio telescope, but except for a few exciting false alarms, no signals showing any kind of artificial patterning were received.

The reader may find the story of Project Ozma anticlimactic. But he should remember that its uniqueness lies in the fact of its having been undertaken at all. Its chances of success were—well, astronomical. Ozma ushered in a new age of scientific endeavor. Similar experiments with more powerful instruments tracking other stars were undertaken shortly afterward in both Green Bank and the Soviet Union. They, too, yielded no results. It is worth mentioning that all these experiments were "passive"—that is, they were efforts to pick up signals arriving from outer space rather than attempts to *send* messages.

Suggestions for a cosmic code

There has also been a great deal of thinking about what to do if and when we receive messages from outer space. The mere ability to send electric impulses into space or pick them up on earth is only half the problem. The other half has all the characteristics of an interdependent decision in absence of direct communication, paradoxically compounded by the fact that the desired outcome is direct communication itself. We have identified a large number of elements common to their first-order reality and to ours. The great question now is how to express these elements; in other words, what code to use.

Since time immemorial the method used to express meaning in the absence of a shared language is by pictorial representation, as in the sign language used to communicate with apes.

At first sight this seems to complicate the problem, for it would seem to be technically easier to send a Morse-type telegram into space than a picture. But it turns out that there is an ingenious way in which the two methods can be combined. Quite naturally, the only "language" a radio telescope can send or receive is based on pulses of electrical energy. Its messages therefore consist of pulses and pauses between pulses. This is a so-called binary code (meaning that it is composed of only two elements, the presence and the absence of the electric pulse), and messages in this code are usually represented as strings of ones and zeros. In a way very similar to that in which an image is produced on a television screen by the very rapid pulses emitted by the TV station, an entire picture can be encoded in binary pulses and sent out by radio waves. In March 1962, Dr. Bernard M. Oliver [119], an expert on information and systems theory, presented to the Institute of Radio Engineers the string of 1,271 units (266 ones and 1,005 zeros), reproduced on the opposite page.° In 1965 this message was selected for inclusion in the time capsule buried at the site of the New York World's Fair to be opened five thousand years hence. Let us review briefly the thinking that went into the construction of the message and that, therefore, holds the key to its decoding.

° A similar but shorter message of 551 units was proposed by Drake in 1961 to the members of the Order of the Dolphins who had participated in the Green Bank radio astronomy conference mentioned on page 172.

266 ones and 1005 zeros. What do they mean?

(see page 186.)

Any terrestrial cryptographer would first examine the message, probably with the aid of a computer, for regularities in the occurrence of the ones, the zeros, or combinations of both. This search would get him nowhere and would suggest to him that the message was probably not composed of words, since none of the frequency distribution analyses, routinely applied to coded language, gave any results. It would be unreasonable for him to assume that his failure was due to the totally alien structure of the language, for as we have seen, there is every reason to believe that the authors of such a message would take the greatest care to make it as simple as possible to decode. Sooner or later our cryptographer would count the elements composing the message, find their number to be 1,271 and begin to wonder what, if anything, this might tell him. Being, of course, trained in number theory, he would remember a fundamental theorem in arithmetic, proved by Ernst Zermelo in 1912, according to which any positive whole number is the unique product of two or more prime numbers.° And just as Gauss had reason to assume that beings out in space would recognize and understand a Pythagorean triangle, our cryptographer would have good reason to believe that the authors of the message, having developed arithmetic, had discovered for themselves the universally valid truth that we call the Zermelo theorem.

Applying this theorem to 1,271, he would find that it was the unique product of 31 × 41. This would inevitably suggest to him the arrangement of the message into a rectangle. Of the two possible arrangements, he might first try the one with a base of 31 units and a height of 41 lines. This would give him a meaningless pattern. But no sooner

° For instance, 105 is the product of the multiplication of the primes 3, 5 and 7, and of no other primes; it is therefore the *unique* product of these three prime numbers.

would he complete the first line of the second arrangement, a rectangle 41 units wide and 31 lines high, with each zero representing an empty space and each number one a dot, than he would realize that this time he might be on the right track, for he finds that this first line has a dot (a one) at the beginning and a dot at the end, and otherwise only zeros. This looks almost like an instruction to subdivide the message into lines of 41 units each. Let us say our cryptographer does just this. Immediately he obtains the picture shown on page 190. With this, his task is accomplished; he will turn over to an astrophysicist what may seem to him an incomprehensible design.°

From an astrophysical point of view, these 1,271 bits of information (as the information theorist would refer to them) turn out to contain a wealth of meaning. The message purports to come from a planet inhabited by erect bipeds like ourselves who reproduce sexually. On the male figure's right is a vertical row of eight symbols, which a cryptographer would easily recognize as the binary numbers† one to eight, read from right to left with a "terminating point" at the end of each number. The entire column seems to refer to the planets in their solar system, with the crude circle at top left obviously representing their sun. The male's right arm points to the fourth distant planet from the sun, presumably indicating that this is where they live. The third planet, the one immediately above, is the starting point of a

---

° This may all sound very complicated, but it is not at all to the expert. Upon receiving the Drake message of 551 bits mentioned in the footnote on page 186, it took Bernard Oliver one hour to decipher it [120].

† In contrast to our ten-digit (decimal) system, the binary system has only two digits, zero and one. It is the simplest number system and the most suitable for the kind of messages we are considering, those composed of pulses (ones) and pauses between pulses (zeros). For a more detailed explanation of the binary system, see any modern handbook of mathematics.

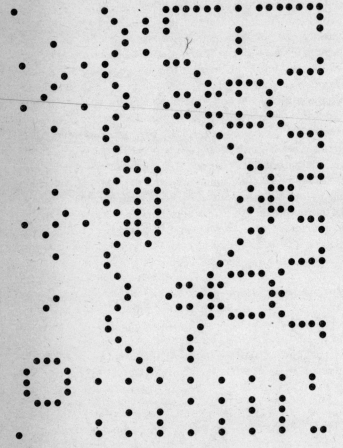

(SEE PAGE 189.)

wave line running horizontally across the diagram. It must be known to these beings to be covered by water and inhabited by organisms that look very much like terrestrial fishes. The diagrams along the top (to the right of the sun) can be recognized as denoting hydrogen, carbon and oxygen atoms, suggesting that the life on this planet is based on a carbohydrate chemistry. The raised hand of the female figure points to the binary number six, perhaps to inform us that they have six fingers and therefore a number system based on twelve (rather than ten, which we with our five fingers have developed). On the right margin, next to the female figure, is what looks like a vertical bracket, indicating the height of the figures, with the binary number eleven close to it. Since so far the only unit of common knowledge to us *and* to them is the 21-cm frequency of their message, it makes sense to assume that they are approximately 11 times 21 cm tall—that is, 221 cm , or $7\frac{1}{2}$ feet. This leads us to the tentative conclusion that they inhabit a planet with slightly lower gravity, and therefore somewhat smaller mass, than ours, permitting them to grow taller than we. They know a good deal about the surface conditions of the planet closest to them (the third from their sun), so presumably they are capable of space travel and may have reached a level of development similar to ours.

Although this message of 1,271 binary units is relatively simple, it contains an astonishing amount of factual information, which in turn leads to a number of additional conclusions° about the reality aspects of their extraterres-

---

° Surprising as this richness may be, it is paltry compared to the mass of explicit and implicit information conveyed by a natural language; for instance, the well-known seven-word dialogue "Gentlemen prefer blondes" . . . "but they marry brunettes." It would require pages and pages to explain its meaning to someone who did not share the many presuppositions of our second-order reality which are condensed into this dialogue.

trial life. What is more, the receipt of this *one* message not only gives us all the factual information just mentioned but also establishes a *method* of communicating, which both they and we can use and refine in our subsequent communications. We have deciphered a cosmic Rosetta Stone, and we now share a code. In other words, the message has important metacommunicational aspects° built into it; it not only communicates information, it also communicates about communication. We and they now literally have a common system of punctuating reality; a rule of communication has emerged in very much the way we discussed on pages 93 ff. But while there we considered the *limitation* inherent in any exchange of messages only in the light of its negative, constricting effects, here the narrowing down of originally infinite possibilities is a very desirable outcome, one that enables us to communicate more and better in subsequent messages.

All of this sounds very neat and plausible, but there is one factor that we briefly mentioned and then conveniently forgot: the enormity of the distances in space. Although these messages will travel with the speed of light, the chances of ever establishing anything even remotely resembling a conversation are minimal. When it comes to interstellar distances, Cade writes,

> any form of personal contact becomes quite impossible. If we assume that the normal working life of an astronomer is forty years, he can ask only one question of his opposite number on a planet twenty light-years away, and even the planets of Tau Ceti or Epsilon Eridani, could only be interrogated twice in a lifetime. With planets at distances of 100 light-years or more, the situation becomes ludicrous; one can perhaps imagine, but never seriously contemplate corre-

° For an introduction to this important concept of metacommunication and its relation to communication, see references 16 and 175.

spondence of the form, "Dear Sir, in reply to the question of your great-great-great-grandfather . . ." [29]

Radioglyphs and Lincos

A sophisticated system for sending messages into space was proposed as early as 1952 by the British scientist Lancelot Hogben in his article "Astroglossa or First Steps in Celestial Syntax." This is not easy reading, but the exposition, all the way from the choice of the first, most obvious signal to the communication of the philosophical concept of self, is extremely lucid. For Hogben, the first step in the celestial syntax, based on what he calls radioglyphs, is the concept of number, just as it was the first step here on earth:

> That people who use multitudinous scripts and languages now employ the same Hindu-Arabic system of numerals reminds us that *number* is the most universal concept by reference to which we can readily establish one-way communication with the first human beings who tried to communicate at a distance through the medium of writing. [72]

Number is the first idiom of reciprocal interstellar understanding, followed by astronomy. Hogben explains that we shall find ourselves in a more difficult situation than a ship-wrecked sailor on an exotic island. He can establish direct communication immediately by pointing to objects and learning the sound symbol (word) which the islanders associate with it. We, on the other hand, first have to devise a technique of how to point at things, and these things will have to be astronomical facts known to the extraterrestrials as well as to us.

An even more complex and comprehensive language for interstellar communication was proposed in 1960 by Professor Hans Freudenthal, a mathematician at the University of Utrecht [45]. He called it *lingua cosmica*, or Lincos. It, too, was designed to be transmitted by radio pulses, and again the first step was the communication of numbers, followed by signs such as $+$, $-$, $=$, introduced by numerical examples. Out of these basic elements Freudenthal developed arithmetic and symbolic logic. The second chapter of his course in Lincos deals with the concept of time, and the third with behavior. In the same crisp, clear, logical progression that characterizes his entire book, he develops the meaning of typical behavior words, like "seeking," "finding," "saying," "counting," of interrogative pronouns, but also of such abstract verbs as "knowing," "perceiving," "understanding," "thinking." At the end of this chapter, Lincos is sufficiently developed to express the paradox of the liar, the man who says of himself, "I am lying"! The fourth chapter deals with space, motion and mass.

Freudenthal is confident that our way of existence and of conceptualizing reality can be taught to extraterrestrials in the same way that we teach children.°

° At the Conference on Communication with Extraterrestrial Intelligence, held in September 1971 at the Byurakan Astrophysical Observatory of the Armenian Academy of Sciences, some general doubts were raised about this assumption. Since they may be of interest to the reader who is trained in mathematical logic, let me briefly mention them in this footnote:

There is reason to suspect that in a very fundamental way, all our attempts to construct a message that, in order to be understood, must communicate its own explanation, will run into the well-known problems of self-reflexivity and, therefore, of paradox. We already encountered this problem when discussing the radio frequency to be used for interstellar communication, and we saw that the communication of this frequency would itself presuppose the very communication we want to establish by its use (page 179). The dog chases its tail. Exactly the same problem is likely to arise when a message is supposed to explain of itself as to how it is to be understood. Ever since Kurt Gödel, then a young mathematician

A message from the year 11,000 B.C.?

During recent years the placement of unmanned space vehicles, mainly communication or observation (spy) satellites, into orbit around the earth has become almost routine. There is no reason why similar probes could not be similarly placed much farther away from our planet either by us or—more likely—by more developed civilizations. According to Professor Ronald N. Bracewell of the Radioscience Laboratory at Stanford University, the advantage of these probes over the methods discussed in the preceding section would be considerable. They would be the work of highly advanced civilizations who would dispatch them into orbit in a star system. The orbit would be chosen in such a way that the spacecraft would circle within the potentially

---

at the University of Vienna, postulated his incompleteness theorem [58], we have known that no system can explain or prove its own consistency without recourse to concepts that the system itself cannot generate but that have to be supplied from the outside by a larger system—which is itself subject to ultimate incompleteness, and so on in an infinite regress of explanation, explanation of explanation, etc. But what is needed here is a message that is complete in itself. This point was raised at the Byurakan conference by the Soviet academicians Idlis and B. N. Panovkin [151].

There is one more intriguing development in this peculiar field of logic. In his book *Laws of Form* [26], George Spencer Brown claims to show that Gödel's proof is not as final and unshakable as it is generally considered to be. To put it in extremely dilettantish terms, Brown purports to have proved that a system can indeed transcend itself (explain itself from the outside, as it were) and then re-enter its own domain, bringing the proof of its consistency with it. (*Laws of Form* is difficult to read, and I have met few people who did not throw up their hands in despair upon reaching the second page. And this in spite of Brown's assurance that his book presupposes "on the part of the reader no more than a knowledge of the English language, of counting and of how numbers are commonly represented" [27].)

life-sustaining distance from that sun. Since for various reasons our solar system is a very eligible target, it is not at all far-fetched to assume that such a probe is already in the vicinity of earth and indeed may have been for a long time, trying to attract our attention. Its primary purpose is presumably simply to "listen" for artificial radiation coming from the planets nearest to it, and either to report its observations automatically back to its home planet or eventually to be "recalled" for the evaluation of the data accumulated in it. Bracewell also considers it possible that these probes could be equipped with sophisticated transmitting equipment, automatically repeating intercepted messages over the same frequency. This would be an excellent and very simple way of making us aware of the existence of the probe and of its innate talents. This is how Bracewell sees things progress from this first contact:

> To notify the probe that we had heard it, we would repeat back to it once again. It would then know that it was in touch with us. After some routine tests to guard against accident, and to test our sensitivity and band-width, it would begin its message, with further occasional interrogation to ensure that it had not set below our horizon. Should we be surprised if the beginning of its message were a television image of a constellation?
>
> These details, and the matter of teaching the probe our language (by transmitting a pictorial dictionary?), are fascinating but present no problems once contact has been made with the probe. The latter is the main problem. The important thing for us is to be alert to the possible interstellar origin of unexpected signals. [21]

Before becoming aware of the existence of the probe, the repetition of our own signals would be very puzzling, for no known facts would account for this radio echo.

Strangely enough, this is exactly what happened in 1927

when a wireless operator in Oslo received the signals of the Dutch shortwave radio station PCJJ at Eindhoven, followed about three seconds later by what was undoubtedly their echo. The matter was investigated, and on October 11, 1928, it was possible to repeat the strange phenomenon by sending out very strong signals from PCJJ and again receiving their echo. This time the echoes were witnessed by Dr. B. van der Pol of the Philips Radio Corporation in Eindhoven and the Norwegian Telegraph Administration in Oslo. The replication was briefly reported in a letter to the journal *Nature* [170] by the principal investigator, the physicist Carl Størmer. Similar echoes were received in subsequent years also by other investigators.

Throughout this book we have repeatedly seen that a state of disinformation, of uncertainty produced by events that do not fit into our definition of reality, has a powerful effect, compelling us to seek an order to account for the disturbing phenomena. The puzzle created by the radio echoes was no exception.

Van der Pol at Eindhoven sent the agreed-upon signal, three dots in rapid succession at thirty-second intervals. Both he and Størmer in Oslo then received a sequence of echoes over exactly the same frequency and with the following delays in seconds: 8, 11, 15, 8, 13, 3, 8, 8, 8, 12, 15, 13, 8, 8. As can be seen, we are here faced with a problem very similar to the one we considered when we were discussing randomness: the question of whether a string of numbers is random or has an internal order. Let us jump a number of intermediate stages and turn directly to the fascinating interpretation of these echoes proposed by Duncan A. Lunan, a graduate of Glasgow University [92]. Greatly condensed, this is what Lunan contends:

The first echoes received in Oslo came three seconds after the original signal, and this went on for more than a year until the experiments in October 1928, when the delays began to vary in length, as shown above. For a signal to return to earth in three seconds, the object producing the echo would have had to be at about the same distance from the earth as our moon. Assuming that Bracewell's suggestion was correct and a probe was circling our planet, this repetition and its three-second delay would mean that the probe was in moon orbit.° If this were all the echo meant to tell us, the sudden variations in the delay times would make no sense. Presumably they marked the beginning of a second phase of communication. This is how Lunan interpreted them:

> It might seem absurd to make up a signal of delay times—like a telegram containing only the word "stop" at varying intervals—but, once thought of, the system has certain advantages for interstellar communication by proxy. It is a more efficient way to send pictures than, for example, a dot-dash sequence in which every dash, or every dot, is to represent a blank square on a grid; and the message carried by variable delay time is less likely to be garbled in transmission. [93]

He then repeated the fruitless attempts that had been tried in 1928 to plot the delay times on the Y (vertical) axis of a graph. Eventually he plotted them on the X (horizontal) axis instead, entering the pulse sequence numbers on the Y axis, and made an interesting discovery:

The eight-second delays divided the graph into two halves. In the right half the delay times greater than eight seconds formed a map of the constellation Boötis, the Herdsman, as seen from earth, with one remarkable omission—the constellation's central star, Epsilon Boötis, was

---

° The plausibility of this assumption is strengthened by the fact that in those years the Eindhoven station was one of the most powerful in continental Europe and therefore a logical target for the supposed probe.

missing. In its stead was the sixth echo of the sequence, the only one with a three-second delay, which fell into the left half of the graph. If this point was rotated 180 degrees around the vertical divider—flipped over from left to right, so to speak—it fell into the exact position of Epsilon Boötis. The conclusion was inescapable: the message showed Boötis, invited us to correct the position of Epsilon Boötis and to send the message back to the probe, thereby signaling that we had learned our second lesson in communication—all of which vindicates Bracewell's prediction that it would not be surprising if a probe's message began with the picture of a constellation.

The most remarkable thing about Lunan's interpretation is that Boötis' brightest star, Alpha Boötis (also known as Arcturus), is not shown where it is today (it has a high degree of proper motion), but where it was 13,000 years ago! In Lunan's opinion, this means that the probe arrived in our solar system sometime in 11,000 B.C. and has been silently circling our planet until the advent of radio in the 1920s, when it became active and started to perform the function for which the extraterrestrials had built it.

Fantastic as all this may seem, too many pieces of the puzzle fall into place for Lunan's hypothesis to be dismissed out of hand. In fact, so convincing is this interpretation that further experiments are now under way to confirm or refute it in all its complex detail, of which this brief description has given only a very superficial idea.

The Pioneer 10 plaque

With the exception of Project Ozma, none of the ideas mentioned so far have been put to a test. But on March 3, 1972, another practical, concrete attempt at interstellar communication was made when Pioneer 10 was launched,

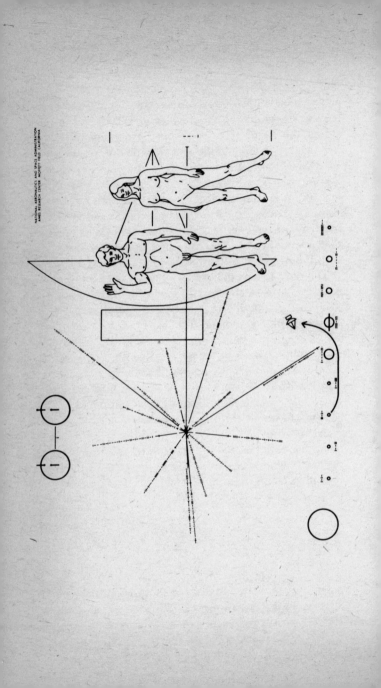

carrying on its outside the 6″ × 9″ gold-plated aluminum plaque shown on page 200.° Pioneer 10 traveled past Jupiter in December 1973 and is now well on its way out of our solar system. Since its course is taking it into a region which, even by outer-space standards, is considered deserted, the chances of its being found are very small. But in the remote event that it is detected and recovered by a spaceship from an advanced galactic civilization, the plaque is supposed to tell these beings something of our world—at least as it was many millions or even billions of years ago.

The most important part of the left half of the drawing is the radial pattern in the center and the data on the bottom. Professor Carl Sagan of Cornell University, the author of this message, explains that the radial lines with their binary encodings would be recognized as

> the characteristic periods of the pulsars, natural and regular sources of cosmic radio emission; pulsars are rapidly rotating neutron stars produced in catastrophic stellar explosions. . . . We believe that a scientifically sophisticated civilization will have no difficulty understanding the radial burst pattern as the positions and periods of 14 pulsars with respect to the Solar System of launch.

But pulsars are cosmic clocks that are running down at largely known rates. The recipients of the message must ask themselves not only where it was ever possible to see 14 pulsars arrayed in such a relative position, but also *when* it was possible to see them. The answers are: Only from a very small volume of the Milky Way Galaxy and in a single year in the history of the Galaxy. Within that small volume there are perhaps a thousand stars; only one is anticipated to have the array of planets with relative distances as indicated at the bottom of the diagram. The rough sizes of the planets

° An identical plaque was sent into space with Pioneer 11 on a similar mission in 1973.

and the rings of Saturn are also schematically shown. A schematic representation of the initial trajectory of the spacecraft launched from Earth and passing by Jupiter is also displayed. Thus, the message specifies one star in about 250 billion and one year (1970) in about 10 billion. [149]

It was the right half of the plaque, however, that provoked the most unexpected and hilarious repercussions here on earth. As the reader may remember, the drawing was published in newspapers all over the world. This resulted in a stream of letters to Sagan (whose wife, incidentally, drew the diagram). Among the more reasonable were those that questioned the meaning of the man's raised arm. Does this gesture have a universal meaning of greeting and good will, they asked, does it signal a threat, or does it mean that the terrestrial man's right arm is permanently angled at the elbow? Other letters suggested that the foreshortening of the feet and other parts of the two figures, so obvious to us earthlings, could lead to strange interpretations by a race unaccustomed to this form of perspective. Then the feminists got into the act and started complaining that the female was represented as much too passive. Finally the nudity of the two figures was attacked. This is all the funnier because in anticipation of puritanical objections, the plaque represents the female as sexless, apparently in a half-hearted attempt to prevent the "worst." That it did not is borne out by a letter to the editor of the Los Angeles *Times*:

> I must say I was shocked by the blatant display of both male and female sex organs on the front page of the *Times*. Surely this type of sexual exploitation is below the standards our community has come to expect from the *Times*.
>
> Isn't it enough that we must tolerate the bombardment of pornography through the media of film and smut magazines?

Isn't it bad enough that our own space agency officials have found it necessary to spread this filth even beyond our own solar system? [150]

In the afternoon of your last day God calls you into His office and tells you what it was all about.

Unimaginable realities

Getting in contact with extraterrestrial intelligence is not really funny at all, and there is no way of even approximately predicting what its effects on mankind will be. The development of intelligent life is certainly not a linear progression. As we saw with apes and dolphins, there are certain critical limits of complexity, for instance of brain organization, and upon reaching these limits, new phenomena suddenly emerge; phenomena that are discontinuous with and therefore not necessarily predictable from the stages of development immediately preceding them. The second-order realities, potentially present out there in space, are unimaginable. Our knowledge about the evolution of our own civilization is so sparse that it is difficult to make even the most modest predictions about stages of psychological, cultural and social evolution on other planets. Mankind has simply not been in existence long enough for us to draw reliable conclusions about the general laws, if any, of the evolution of civilizations.°

° This is borne out by the work of the Club of Rome, an international body of experts studying the socioeconomic development of our planet. In spite of highly sophisticated, computer-based projections, it seems almost impossible to go much beyond the year 2000, and 2100 is the limit of even tentative predictability.

In spite of these difficulties, a great deal of painstaking work on the probability of cultures on other planets has been done by Soviet

If the entire life of our planet, from its origin to the present moment, were represented by a twenty-four-hour day, intelligent life appeared within the last few seconds. As we succeed in digging more and more deeply into our own past, into those long hours preceding the last few seconds, we learn increasingly more about the laws governing the development of life under the physical conditions prevailing by and large throughout our galaxy. And as we have said, we have reason to believe that the blueprints of life on other planets will not differ too much from our own. As the authors of Project Cyclops put it:

> Regardless of the morphology of other intelligent beings, their microscopes, telescopes, communication systems, and power plants must have been at some time in their history, almost indistinguishable in working principles from ours. To be sure there will be differences in the order of invention and application of techniques and machines, but technological systems are shaped more by the physical laws of optics, thermodynamics, electromagnetics, or atomic reactions on which they are based, than by the nature of the beings that design them. A consequence of this is that we need not worry much over the problem of exchanging information between biological forms of separate origin. For we share with any intelligence we might contact a large base of technology, scientific knowledge, and mathematics that can be used to build up a language for conveying subtler concepts. [137]

It also seems reasonable to assume that this (probably rather one-sided) exchange of information will be very helpful; occasionally the view is expressed that through it we will find the answers to such problems as cancer,

---

scientists. It is available to the English-speaking reader in Kaplan's *Extraterrestrial Civilizations* [78] (see especially chapters V and VI).

controlled nuclear reaction or the population explosion. However, the results may also be entirely different.°

There's the rub. As Bracewell points out, the mortality rate for advanced civilizations may be too high for them to become abundant in the galaxy [21]. Overpopulation, pollution, nuclear accident or increasing moral retardation may well be the death symptoms of *any* (and therefore also our) civilization. Perhaps we are dinosaurs.†

Even if this is not the case, it is difficult to share the great euphoria about the expected benefits of contact with extraterrestrials. While we can fairly safely dismiss the science-fiction notion of an invasion of our planet by fiendish beings from outer space, nothing is certain about the psychological and social impact upon us of information from much more advanced civilizations. The only possible analogy we have from developments within our own terrestrial world is the disastrous effect of our progress on "primitive" cultures like the Australian aborigines, the Eskimos and the Brazilian Indios. We have already reached

---

° In fairness to the authors of Project Cyclops, it should be pointed out that they have few illusions about the predictability of the exchange:

> About all that can be said for sure about such prophecies is that, however stimulating they may be, they are almost certainly all wrong. To become convinced of this we need merely observe how unpredictable our own progress has been over the last two millennia. What ancient Greek or Alexandrian would have predicted the dark ages, the discovery of the new world, or the atomic era? Who among the ancients, wise as they were in many ways, would have forecast the automobile, television, antibiotics, or the modern computer? To Aristotle, the fact that men could do sums was proof that they had souls. Yet here we sit attempting predictions about worlds not two thousand but hundreds of thousands or even millions of years beyond us, and of independent origin at that! [138]

† In the above-mentioned article, Bracewell speculates that "such communities [i.e., advanced civilizations] may be collapsing at the rate of two a year (10^3 in 500 years) . . ."

a stage where our scientific and technological advances have left our moral maturity far behind. The sudden availability of vastly superior knowledge, propelling our thinking thousands of years ahead without benefit of a coherent, gradual acquisition of all the intermediate steps leading to these results, might have truly staggering consequences. Clinical experience teaches us that sudden exposure to information of overwhelming magnitude has one of two effects: the victim either closes his mind to the new reality and behaves as if it did not exist, or he takes leave of reality altogether. The latter is the essence of madness.

18
Imaginary Communication

Throughout this book we have concerned ourselves with realities of an increasingly imaginary nature—from the practical, concrete vicissitudes of language translation and psychological experiments to philosophical problems and finally to speculations about extraterrestrial realities.

In this last section I want to present examples of communication contexts that are purely imaginary but at the same time lead to intriguing, albeit contradictory conclusions. My license for doing this is the same as the mathematician's; his business, as Nagel and Newman once stated, "is to derive theorems from postulated assumptions," and "it is not his concern as a mathematician to decide whether the axioms he assumes are actually true" [116].

Étienne de Condillac, the eighteenth-century philosopher and economist, used to outline what was to become the basis of so-called association psychology by postulating an at-first inanimate statue, which became more and more human as he imagined it to be increasingly endowed with perceptual capabilities. But the classic example is Maxwell's Demon, an imaginary tiny doorkeeper who controls the connection between two containers filled with the same gas. The molecules of any gas bounce around randomly and at different speeds. The Demon uses his little door to allow the free passage of any molecule that comes shooting from container A into container B, but quickly closes the door whenever a molecule tries to bounce from B into A. Gradually, therefore, container A is filled with most of the fast-moving molecules, while B contains the slow (low energy) ones. As a result of this discrimination by the Demon, the temperature in container A rises while B gets colder, although they both started out with the same internal temperature. This, however, contradicts the Second Law of Thermodynamics. Although the entire matter was "only" an intellectual exercise, it greatly bothered theoretical physicists for a long time. Maxwell's Paradox, as it became known, was eventually resolved by the physicist Leon Brillouin, who, on the basis of a paper by Szilard, showed that the Demon's observation of the molecules amounted to an increase of information within the system, an increase that had to be paid for by exactly the amount of energy the Demon generated. Thus, while to laymen the entire idea of Maxwell's Demon seems absurd, it led physicists to important insights into the interdependence of energy and information.

Newcomb's Paradox

Every once in a while the long list of paradoxes is enriched by a new, particularly intriguing, mind-boggling one, like the Prisoner's Dilemma or the prediction paradox, mentioned in the footnote on page 129, both of which generated a vast literature.

In 1960, a theoretical physicist at the Livermore Radiation Laboratories of the University of California, Dr. William Newcomb, hit upon yet another, reportedly while trying to sort out the Prisoner's Dilemma. Through various intermediaries it eventually reached Harvard University philosopher Robert Nozick, who published it in a truly mind-bending paper in 1970 [118]. In 1973 it was reviewed by Martin Gardner in *Scientific American* [53] and produced such a flood of readers' letters that Gardner, after consulting with Nozick, published a column, with a second article on the subject by Nozick [54].

This paradox is based on communication with an imaginary Being; a Being that has the ability to predict human choices with *almost* total accuracy. As Nozick defines the Being's ability (and the reader is urged to pay attention to his definition, since it is indispensable to the understanding of what is to follow): "You know that this Being has often correctly predicted your choices in the past (and has never, so far as you know, made an incorrect prediction about your choices), and furthermore you know that this Being has often correctly predicted the choices of other people, many of whom are similar to you, in the particular situation to be described below."

The Being shows you two boxes and explains that Box 1 contains $1,000, while Box 2 contains either $1 million or nothing. You have two choices: to take what is in both boxes, or to take only what is in the second box. The Being has arranged the following outcomes: if you choose alternative 1 and take what is in both boxes, the Being (predicting this) will leave Box 2 empty; you therefore get only $1,000. If you decide to take only Box 2, the Being (predicting this) puts the $1 million in it. This is the sequence of events: the

Being makes his prediction, *then* (depending on his prediction of your choice), he either does or does not put the $1 million in Box 2, *then* he communicates the conditions to you, *then* you make your choice. You fully understand the conditions, the Being knows you understand them, you know that he knows, and so on—exactly as in the other interdependent contexts that we examined in Part II.

The beauty of this imaginary situation is that there are two equally possible and equally plausible but totally contradictory outcomes. What is more, as Newcomb quickly found and as the deluge of letters Gardner received amply demonstrated, one of the choices will immediately appear to you the "obvious" and "logical" one and you will not for the life of you understand how anybody could possibly even consider the other. Yet a very strong argument can be made for either strategy, and this throws us back into a reality "where everything is true, and so is its contrary."

According to the first argument, you can have almost complete confidence in the Being's predictive ability. Therefore, if you decide to take both boxes, the Being will almost certainly have predicted this and will have left Box 2 empty. But if you decide to take only what is in the second box, the Being will almost certainly have predicted this choice as well and will have put the $1 million in it. So it obviously makes sense to choose only Box 2. Where is the problem?

The problem lies in the logic of the second argument. Remember that the Being makes his prediction first, then tells you the conditions, and *then* you decide. This means that by the time you make your decision, the $1 million *is already in the second box or it is not.* Ergo, if it is in Box 2, and you elect to take what is in both boxes, you get $1,001,000. But if Box 2 is empty and you take both boxes, you get at least the $1,000 from Box 1. In either case you get $1,000 *more* by choosing both boxes than by taking only what is in Box 2. The inescapable conclusion is that you should decide to open both boxes.

Oh no, the supporters of the first argument are quick to point out: It is this very reasoning that the Being has (almost certainly) predicted correctly and has therefore left Box 2 empty.

You don't get our point, the defenders of the second argument reply: The Being has made his prediction and the $1 million now is (or is not) in Box 2. No matter what you decide, the money has already been there (or not been there) for an hour, a day or a week *before* you made your decision. Your decision is not going to make it disappear if it is already in Box 2, nor will it make it suddenly appear in Box 2 as a result of your decision to take only what is in Box 2. You make the mistake of believing that there is some sort of "backward causality" involved—that your decision will make the $1 million appear or disappear, as the case may be. But the money is already there or not there *before* you make up your mind. In either case it would be foolish to take only Box 2; for if Box 2 is filled, why forgo the $1,000 in Box 1? If Box 2 turns out to be empty, you will certainly want to win at least the $1,000.

Nozick invites the reader to try this paradox on friends and students, and he predicts that they will divide fairly evenly into proponents of the two contradictory arguments. Moreover, most of them will think that the others are silly. But, Nozick warns, "it will not do to rest with one's belief that one knows what to do. Nor will it do to just repeat one of the arguments, loudly and slowly." Quite correctly, he demands that one must pursue the other argument until its absurdity becomes evident. This, however, nobody has so far succeeded in doing.

It is possible—but has not, to the best of my knowledge, been previously suggested—that this dilemma, like some of the contradictions and paradoxes which we will examine in the section on time travel, is based on a fundamental confusion between two very distinct meanings of the apparently unambiguous proposition *if-then*. In the sentence "If Tom is the father of Bob, then Bob is the son of Tom," the *if-then* signifies a timeless logical relationship between the two. But in the statement "If you press this button, then the bell will ring," the relationship is a purely causal one, and all causal relationships are temporal in the sense that there is of necessity a time lag between cause and effect, be it only the millisecond needed by the electric current to flow from the button to the bell.

It may well be that people defending the first argument (to take only what is in Box 2) are reasoning on the basis of the logical, timeless meaning of *if-then*: "If I decide to take only what is in Box 2, then the box contains a million dollars." The supporters of the second argument (to take what is in both boxes) appear to be reasoning on the basis of the causal, temporal *if-then*: "if the Being has *already* made his prediction, then he has accordingly put, or not put, the million in Box 2, and in either case I get a thousand dollars more if I take what is in both boxes." As the reader can see, the second argument is based on the causal time sequence: prediction—(non)placement of the money—my choice. In this perspective my choice comes *after* both the Being's prediction of my choice and his subsequent (non)placement of the money, and my choice cannot exert any backward influence over what took place *before* it.

This possible solution of Newcomb's Paradox and of some of the puzzles contained in the section on time requires a thorough examination from first principles that I am alas incompetent to perform but that may provide an interesting challenge to a graduate student of philosophy.

At this point several strands left dangling in the pages of this book begin to converge into a discernible texture. We have seen that the question of whether or not our reality has an order is of the greatest importance and that there are three possible answers:

1. It has no order, in which case reality is tantamount to *confusion* and chaos, and life would be a psychotic nightmare.

2. We relieve our existential state of *disinformation* by inventing an order, forget that we have invented it and experience it as something "out there" which we call reality.

3. There is an order. It is the creation of some higher Being on whom we depend but who itself is quite independent of us. *Communication* with this Being, therefore, becomes man's most important goal.

Most of us manage to ignore possibility 1. But none of us can avoid making some sort of commitment—no matter how vague or unconscious—for either possibility 2 or 3. As I see it, this is what the Newcomb Paradox drives home so forcefully: you either believe that reality, and with it the course of events, is rigidly, inescapably ordered, as defined by possibility 3, in which case you take only what is in Box 2, or you subscribe to possibility 2—you believe that you can decide independently, that your decision is not predetermined, that there is no "backward causality" (making future events determine the present or even the past), and take what is in both boxes.

As Gardner has pointed out, this amounts to a restatement of the age-old controversy over determinism versus free will. And this innocent little mind game suddenly throws us into one of the oldest unsolved problems of philosophy.

What the problem boils down to is this: When faced with the everyday necessity of making a choice, any choice, how do I choose? If I really believe that my choice, like any other event, is determined by (is the inescapable effect of) all the causes in the past, then the idea of free will or free choice is an illusion. It does not matter how I choose, for whatever I choose is the only thing I *can* choose. There are no alternatives, and even if I think there are, this thought itself is nothing but the effect of some cause in my personal past. Whatever happens to me and whatever I myself do is predetermined by something that, depending on my preference (oops—I mean, of course, depending on some inescapable cause in my past) I may call causality,° the Being, the divine experimenter or fate.

If I really believe that my will is free, then I live in a totally different reality. I am the master of my fate, and what I do here and now creates my reality.

Unfortunately both views are untenable, and nobody, no matter how "loudly and slowly" he makes his case for one or the other, can live by it. If everything is strictly determined, what is the use of trying, of taking risks, how can I be held responsible for my actions, what about morals and ethics? The outcome is fatalism, which itself suffers from a fatal paradox: to embrace this view of reality one must make a nonfatalistic decision—one must decide in what amounts to a *free act of choice* that whatever happens is fully determined and that there is no freedom of choice.

But if I am the captain of my ship, if I am not determined by past causes, if I can freely make my decisions—then what on earth do I base them on? On a randomizer in my head, as Gardner so aptly puts it? We have already had a

---

° The scientific concept that comes closest to Newcomb's Being is, of course, causality, a very high statistical probability of outcome: if I release my pen in midair, it will fall to the floor. I expect this because on all previous occasions it (or any other object, for that matter) has always fallen and it has never (with me or anybody else, as far as I know) shot up to the ceiling. But according to modern scientific theory, there is absolutely no guarantee that the next time it will not do just that. If we compare Nozick's definition of the Being with this definition of causality, the similarity is evident.

taste of the weird troubles with randomness, which turned out to be just as unsettling as those connected with the idea of a divine experimenter.

There does not seem to be an answer, although many have been offered in the course of the past two thousand years, from Heraclitus and Parmenides to Einstein. To mention just a few of the more modern ones: for Leibniz the world is a huge clockwork, wound up once and for all by God and now ticking away into eternity, with not even the divine clockmaker himself able to alter its course. So why worship this God if He Himself is powerless to influence His own creation, causality? This, in essence, is the same as the paradox described on page 15: God is caught by His own rules; either He cannot create a rock too heavy to lift Himself, or He cannot lift it—in either case He is not omnipotent. Laplace is the most famous advocate of the extreme deterministic view:

> We ought then to regard the present state of the universe as the effect of its anterior state and as the cause of the one which is to follow. Given for one instant an intelligence which could comprehend all the forces by which nature is animated and the respective situation of the beings who compose it—an intelligence sufficiently vast to submit these data to analysis—it would embrace in the same formula the movements of the greatest bodies of the universe and those of the lightest atom; for it, nothing would be uncertain and the future, as the past, would be present to its eyes. [85]

There is no biographical evidence that Laplace based his own life on this world view and reached the logical conclusion, fatalism. In fact, he was a very active, creative scientist and philosopher, deeply concerned with social improvements. Monod, as we have seen (pages 82–83), attempts the solution on the basis of the complementarity of chance and necessity. And in a lecture at the University of Göttingen in July 1946, the famous physicist Max Planck suggested a way out of the dilemma by postulating a duality of viewpoints: the external, or scientific, and the internal, or volitional. As he summarized it in a subsequent publication, the controversy of free will versus determinism is a phantom problem:

> . . . We can therefore say: Observed from without, the will is causally determined. Observed from within, it is free. This finding takes care of the problem of the freedom of the will. This problem came into being because people were not careful enough to specify explicitly the viewpoint of the observation, and to adhere to it consistently. This is a typical example of a phantom problem. Even though this truth is still being disputed time and again, there is no doubt in my mind that it is but a question of time before it will gain universal recognition. [129]

Thirty years have passed since this was written, but there is no sign that it has gained universal recognition as a resolution of the free-will dilemma. If it is a phantom problem, Planck seems to have given it a phantom solution.

Dostoevski, on the other hand, attempts no solution. He places the dilemma squarely before our eyes: Jesus and the Grand Inquisitor represent free will and determinism, respectively, and they are both right and both wrong. When all is said and done, we find ourselves where Ivan Karamazov's poem finishes—unable to follow either Jesus' "Be spontaneous" paradox of free compliance or the deceptive illusion deliberately imposed by the Grand Inquisitor. What we do instead and will continue to do every day of our lives is to ignore both horns of the dilemma by blunting our minds to the eternal contradiction and living as if it did not exist. The outcome is that strange affliction called "mental health" or, funnier still, "reality adaptation."

Flatland

Almost a hundred years ago the headmaster of the City of London School, the Reverend Edwin A. Abbott, wrote a small, unimposing book. He was a classics scholar, and his works—over forty in number—deal mostly with the classics or with religion. But, to borrow James Newman's pithy remark [117], "his only hedge against oblivion" is that little book with the title *Flatland: A Romance in Many Dimensions* [1].

While *Flatland* is written in, shall we say, a rather flat style, it is nevertheless a unique book, not only because it anticipates some developments of modern theoretical physics but because of its astute psychological intuition which the heaviness of its Victorian style fails to squelch. I have often wished that it, or a modernized version, would be made required reading in high schools.

Flatland is told by an inhabitant of a two-dimensional world—that is, it has length and breadth but no height—a world as flat as a sheet of paper covered with lines, triangles, squares, etc. The people move around freely on or, rather, in this surface, but like shadows, they are unable to rise above or sink below that plane. Needless to say, they are unaware of this inability; the existence of a third dimension—height—is unimaginable to them.

The narrator has a mind-shattering experience preceded by a strange dream. In his dream he is transferred to Lineland, a one-dimensional world where all the beings are either lines or points, moving to and fro on the same straight line. This line is what they call space, and the idea of moving to the left or right of this "space," instead of merely to and fro, is totally unimaginable to the Linelanders. In vain the dreamer tries to explain to the longest line in

Lineland (the monarch) what Flatland is like. The King considers him deluded, and the narrator eventually loses his patience:

> Why waste more words? Suffice it that I am the completion of your incomplete self. You are a line, but I am a Line of Lines, called in my country a Square: and even I, infinitely superior though I am to you, am of little account among the great nobles of Flatland, whence I have come to visit you, in the hope of enlightening your ignorance. [2]

Upon hearing these mad insults, the King and all his line- and point-shaped subjects prepare to launch an attack on the Square, who at this moment is awakened to the realities of Flatland by the sound of the breakfast bell.

In the course of the day, another disconcerting event takes place. The Square is teaching his little grandson, a Hexagon,° some basic notions of arithmetic as applied to geometry. He shows him how the number of square inches in a square can be computed by simply elevating the number of inches of one side to its second power:

> The little Hexagon meditated on this a while and then said to me, "But you have been teaching me to raise numbers to the third power: I suppose 3^3 must mean something in Geometry; what does it mean?" "Nothing at all," replied I, "not at least in Geometry; for Geometry has only Two Dimensions." And then I began to shew the boy how a Point by moving through a length of three inches makes a Line of three inches, which may be represented by 3; and how a Line of three inches, moving parallel to itself through a

---

° As the narrator explains, it is a law of nature in Flatland that a male child always has one more side than his father, provided the father is at least a Square and not merely a lowly Triangle. When the number of the sides becomes so great that the figure can no longer be distinguished from a circle, the person is a member of the Circular or Priestly Order.

length of three inches, makes a Square of three inches every way, which may be represented by 3^2.

Upon this, my Grandson, again returning to his former suggestion, took me up rather suddenly and exclaimed, "Well, then, if a Point, by moving three inches, makes a Line of three inches represented by 3; and if a straight Line of three inches, moving parallel to itself, makes a Square of three inches every way, represented by 3^2; it must be that a Square of three inches every way, moving somehow parallel to itself (but I don't see how), must make Something else (but I don't see what) of three inches every way—and this must be represented by 3^3."

"Go to bed," said I, a little ruffled by this interruption: "if you would talk less nonsense, you would remember more sense." [3]

Thus the Square, paying no attention to the lesson he might have drawn from his dream, repeats exactly the same mistake he tried so hard to point out to the King of Lineland. But as the evening progresses he cannot quite shake off the prattle of the little Hexagon, and eventually exclaims aloud, "The boy is a fool, I say; 3^3 can have no meaning in geometry." At once he hears a voice: "The boy is not a fool; and 3^3 has an obvious geometrical meaning." The voice belongs to a strange visitor who claims to have come from Spaceland—an unimaginable universe in which things have three dimensions. The visitor tries to make the Square see what three-dimensional reality is like and how limited Flatland is by comparison. And just as the Square introduced himself to the King of Lineland as a Line of Lines, the visitor defines himself as a Circle of Circles, called a Sphere in Spaceland. This, of course, the Square cannot grasp, for all he sees of his visitor is a circle—but a circle with most disturbing, unexplainable properties: it waxes and wanes in diameter, occasionally shrinking to a mere point and disappearing altogether. Very patiently the

Sphere explains that there is nothing strange about this: He is an infinite number of circles, varying in size from a point to a circle of thirteen inches in diameter, placed one on top of the other. When he passes through the two-dimensional reality of Flatland, he is at first invisible to a Flatlander, then—upon touching the plane of Flatland—he appears as a point; as he continues, he looks like a circle, constantly growing in diameter, until he begins to shrink and eventually disappears again (see diagram).

Flatland ———————————————————————————————→ Perspective of the Square

The Sphere passing through Flatland

This also explains how the Sphere managed to enter the Square's two-dimensional house despite its locked doors—he simply stepped into it from above. But the idea of "from above" is so alien to the Square's reality that he cannot fathom it. And since he cannot, he refuses to believe it. Finally the Sphere sees no other recourse than to produce in the Square what we would nowadays call a transcendental experience:

An unspeakable horror seized me. There was a darkness; then a dizzy, sickening sensation of sight that was not like seeing; I saw a Line that was no Line; Space that was not Space: I was myself, and not myself. When I could find voice, I shrieked aloud in agony, "Either this is madness or it is Hell." "It is neither," calmly replied the voice of the Sphere, "it is Knowledge; it is Three Dimensions: open your eye once again and try to look steadily." [4]

But from this mystical moment on, things take a humorous turn. Intoxicated with the overwhelming experience of stepping into this totally new reality, the Square is now eager to discover the mysteries of higher and higher worlds, of "more spacious space, some more dimensionable dimensionality," the land of four, five and six dimensions. But the Sphere will have none of this trifling: "There is no such land. The very idea of it is utterly inconceivable." Since the Square will not stop insisting on the point, the infuriated Sphere eventually throws him back into the narrow confines of Flatland.

At this point the moral of the story becomes sadly realistic. The Square sees a glorious career before him: to go forth at once and evangelize the whole of Flatland, proclaiming the Gospel of Three Dimensions. But not only does it become increasingly difficult for him to remember exactly what he perceived in three-dimensional reality, he is eventually arrested and tried by the Flatland equivalent of the Inquisition. Rather than being burned, he is sentenced to perpetual imprisonment under circumstances which the author's uncanny intuition makes sound very much like certain mental hospitals today. Once a year the Chief Circle—that is, the High Priest—comes to visit him in his cell and asks him if he is feeling any better. And every year the poor Square cannot refrain from trying again to convince him that there *is* such a thing as a third dimension. Whereupon the Chief Circle shakes his head and leaves for another year.

What *Flatland* brilliantly depicts is the utter relativity of reality. Perhaps the most murderous element in human history is the delusion of a "real" reality, with all the consequences that logically follow from it. On the other hand, it requires a very high degree of maturity and tolerance for others to live with relative truth, with questions for which there are no answers, with the knowledge that one knows nothing and with the uncertainties produced by paradox. Yet if we cannot develop this ability, we will, without knowing it, relegate ourselves to the Grand Inquisitor's world, in which we will live the lives of sheep, occasionally troubled by the acrid smoke rising from some auto-da-fé or the chimneys of crematoria.

19

Time Travel

> *It is only another way of looking
> at Time. There is no difference
> between Time and any of the three
> dimensions of Space except that
> our consciousness moves along it.*
>
> —H. G. Wells, *The Time Machine*

In summer you can board Alitalia flight no. 338, leaving Rome at 14.05 hours (2.05 P.M.) and arrive in Nice at precisely the same time. In other words, you have traveled forward in space and backward in time. Upon arrival in Nice you are an hour older than your friends who are meeting you—you are a Rip Van Winkle in reverse.

The event is trivial. It is possible because on the first Sunday in June, Italy is the only European country to go from Central European time to daylight saving time. The hour that everyone in Italy thus "saves," he "loses" as he leaves the country. And you lost this hour on the plane because Alitalia's DC-9 covers the distance from Rome to Nice in exactly one hour.

The two U.S. Air Force officers who flew their SR-71 from the Farnborough air show near London to California in September 1974 did even better. They arrived over Los Angeles more than four hours *before* they left London. Again, of course, the feat is possible only because London and Los Angeles are located in different time zones, a fact known to every air traveler (and his physiology).

Such seemingly simple and obvious concepts as *before, at the same time* and *after*, which I have used freely here, are intimately related to our everyday experience of time and its three aspects: past, present and future. And everything is fine as long as we use the words on a common-sense level, which rests on the cozy mirage of a simple, consistent reality. But every once in a while we are brutally reminded that our common sense is based not on wisdom but on that old recipe: If you don't look, it will go away. It may not go away, especially not if "it" is the painful, guilt-provoking consequence of a wrong decision. To be able to foresee the future is one of mankind's oldest, fondest dreams—and not only that of the man playing roulette or the stock market.

As we move with time, we constantly find ourselves at the line dividing future from past. Our most immediate experience of reality, the present, is merely that infinitesimally short moment at which the future becomes the past. It is also the instant when the properties of reality are somehow turned upside down: the future is changeable but not known; the past is known but not changeable.° Or, as the French put it, *"Si jeunesse savait, si vieillesse pouvait!"* (If youth only knew, if age only could). Small wonder that philosophers and poets have at times attributed the Creation to the mockery of a spiteful demiurge, constantly

---

° I am, of course, oversimplifying. There are many things that can be predicted very accurately—for instance, planetary motions, the tides of the oceans, chemical and physical events, the fact that if I don't step on my brakes I shall run over that pedestrian, etc. But notice that awareness of these aspects of our first-order reality does very little toward relieving the general uncertainty of life.

demanding our right decisions while leaving us in the dark and showing us what we should have done only when it is too late to do it.

Pseudophilosophical as these considerations may be, they nonetheless indicate that our experience of time is intimately linked with the idea of causality. When we say that one event is the cause of another, we obviously mean that the second event follows the first in time. (This is again the temporal *if-then*, which we must carefully distinguish from the timeless *if-then* of logic.) It would be quite absurd to think that the sequence of events could also be the other way around: that an event in the future could cause another event in the past. Planned action makes sense only because, as far as we know, time flows in only one direction, and we assume that our entire universe is moving with it at the same pace. Otherwise objects traveling at a different "time speed" would disappear into the past or the future, as the case might be. But they do not, and this suggests that the explanation given by H. G. Wells's time traveler, who is quoted at the beginning of this chapter, is correct.

Time is *not*, as it is sometimes believed to be, merely a dimension of the human mind, a necessary delusion of consciousness. And indeed, physics has found evidence of this. Einstein's and Minkowski's space-time continuum is the most modern and precise representation of our physical reality yet presented, and it leaves no doubt that our universe is four-dimensional, although the fourth dimension, time, has properties quite different from those shared by the three spatial dimensions. Above all, it is not as directly accessible to our senses. But we can at least appreciate that four types of measurements are needed to define the location of an event in our world—its spatial coordinates (e.g., longitude, latitude and elevation) and its point in time. Beyond this modest degree of understanding we are not much better off than the Square in Flatland was when the

Sphere tried to explain to him the properties of three-dimensional reality.

Let us return once more to the illustration on page 220 and assume that the eye on the right margin of the diagram is our own. Let us further assume that the sphere descending from above and passing through the two-dimensional space of Flatland is somehow representative of time. Just as the Square could not comprehend the properties of the Sphere in its totality but could perceive only individual circular cross sections of the infinite number of such cross sections composing a sphere, each having only an infinitesimal height, so we in our three-dimensional world cannot perceive time in its totality, but only the infinitesimally short instances of the present. What came before, we call the past, and what is yet to follow, the future, but the sum total of the phenomenon time (in which past, present and future coexist) is as unimaginable to us as the idea of a sphere was to the Square.

Suppose that a person's life has been filmed in its entirety, from birth to death or, if you prefer, from his appearance in time to his disappearance (we shall disregard the fact that his cells anteceded and outlived him), and that we have this film before us, wound on a large reel. Since the film contains the person's whole life, all events are there, coexisting without any temporal order. (Let us, please, disregard the fact that the analogy is not quite satisfactory, because the person's birth will be located at the beginning, the outside, of the film, while his later experiences will be closer and closer to the center of the reel.)

If we run the film through a projector, temporal order is restored, and the events of the person's life unfold in the order in which he experienced them. But to us observers there is no getting away from the fact that his entire life is there on the film, and that every single picture of the film is past, present or future, depending upon whether it has already run through the projector, is at this very instant in front of the lens, or is still on the feed reel. The film itself, without the motion introduced by the projector, is the analogy of a timeless universe, which the Greek philosopher Parmenides defined as "whole and unique, and immovable, and without end; nor was it ever, nor will it be, since it is now all at once, one, continuous" [121].

This is a far cry from what Reichenbach appropriately calls the *emotive* significance of time. All of us have seen a moving picture or read a book more than once and been fascinated the second time as if we did not already know the outcome of every event. "What we regard as Becoming," Reichenbach writes,

> is merely our acquisition of knowledge of the future, but it has no relevance to the happenings themselves. The following story, which was told to me as true, may illustrate this conception. In a moving-picture version of *Romeo and Juliet*, the dramatic scene was shown in which Juliet, seemingly dead, is lying in the tomb, and Romeo, believing she is dead, raises a cup containing poison. At this moment an outcry from the audience was heard: "Don't do it!" We laugh at the person who, carried away by the emotion of subjective experience, forgets that the time flow of a movie is unreal, is merely the unwinding of a pattern imprinted on a strip of film. Are we more intelligent than this man when we believe that the time flow of our actual life is different? Is the present more than our cognizance of a predetermined pattern of events unfolding itself like an unwinding film? [141]

This question throws us back into the dilemma of Newcomb's Paradox. All we have to do is imagine that the Being can predict future events because he has solved the problem of time travel. He travels into the future, looks at your decision regarding the two boxes, comes back to the present and either puts or does not put the $1 million in Box 2. For him, the time traveler, time is merely a long film strip which he can examine at any point he chooses. But if time is merely the unwinding of a film, we are back at complete determinism, and all free choice is an illusion. On the other hand, if time unfolds freely, if every moment is pregnant with all the conceivable possibilities of choice, then there is an infinite number of universes—and that, in itself, is an unimaginable reality. If this is the case, we are living in a Magic Theater like the one in Hermann Hesse's *Steppenwolf*, with an infinite number of doors to choose from. But how do we choose? With that "randomizer in our head"?

Again we have come full circle. If only we could travel into the future and see for ourselves! But wait—what difference would that make? If all our actions and outcomes are already there, our foreknowledge of them would not change them in the least; we would be in the horrible position of *having to make* the very same choices that we now *know* are wrong and will be damaging to us or others. Would we not prefer to return to our merciful state of ignorance? What hell life would be if, for instance, we knew the date and the circumstances of our death.

But assume that after having traveled into the future and returned to the present, we *can* decide on a different course of action. Would this different action not perforce produce a different future of which we would again be ignorant? In other words, wouldn't our foreknowledge irreversibly change reality, again in ways that we cannot foresee unless we also travel into *that* future and thereby repeat the whole cycle? °

° A rather weak analogy to this problem is the law in various countries that election results may not be made public by the news media before all the polls are closed, especially those in the westernmost states or provinces, if the country has various time zones. The reason for this is the

What if the future of which we have gained precognition concerns another person? Are we going to communicate it to him, and what results will this communication have? People who believe that they have this kind of "second sight" are usually troubled by this problem. Even if the soothsayer is a fake, his wrong predictions may very well become self-fulfilling prophecies, not because they correctly predict the future, but because *their having been made changes the future.*° In other words, as long as the other person believes in predictions, it does not really matter whether they are correct or not in an abstract sense, for they will affect that person's behavior just as powerfully and irreversibly as a "real" prophecy. (This leads us into further problems of human interaction that I prefer to leave to the reader's imagination.)

But wouldn't foreknowledge enable us to create an almost ideal world? For instance, we could save thousands of lives by evacuating an area we knew would be devastated by an earthquake on a certain date. We could prevent bad cause-effect relationships from taking place. It would, for example, be perfectly easy not to let oneself be bitten by a particular mosquito at a particular moment and thereby prevent oneself from contracting malaria.

In one of his science-fiction novels, *The End of Eternity*, Isaac Asimov considers the fallacy of this seemingly blissful

---

realization that voting decisions can be influenced by the voters' knowledge (which they get via radio or TV) of the trends produced by the votes *already* cast. In a certain sense, then, the person about to vote would have a "foreknowledge" which the voters who had *already* cast their votes did not and could not have.

° This mechanism is known to every speculator on the stock market. If a widely read publication like the *Wall Street Journal* makes a favorable earnings prediction about a certain company, that company's stock is likely to go up the same day, simply because many people now think that other people will think that the stock is going to go up and will buy it.

state of affairs. Mankind has developed time travel, can observe future events and is thus in a position to prevent undesirable outcomes by simply interfering with the causal chains leading to them, in very small, harmless ways which, however, have very decisive consequences in the distant future. The hero, Andrew Harlan, graduates to this preventive technicianhood by a correctly planned intervention: he jams the clutch of a student's car and thereby makes it impossible for the young man to get to a lecture on mechanics he had meant to attend. This insignificant event of missing the first class, however, makes him lose interest in the subject and thus becomes responsible for his decision not to study solar engineering, and as a result a war that would otherwise have taken place in the next century "is moved out of reality." What could be more desirable and humane?

But toward the end of the novel, the heroine summarizes the disastrous results of this utopia, which is called Eternity:

> In ruling out the disasters of Reality, Eternity rules out the triumphs as well. It is in meeting the great tests that mankind can most successfully rise to great heights. Out of danger and restless insecurity comes the force that pushes mankind to newer and loftier conquests. Can you understand that? Can you understand that in averting the pitfalls and miseries that beset man, Eternity prevents men from finding their own bitter and better solutions, the real solutions that come from conquering difficulty, not avoiding it? [12]

I am afraid not too many people will understand her point of view. Even in this day and age it is considered evil and reactionary to point to the totalitarian consequences of this sort of bliss and to the pathologies of the utopia syndrome [184].

The chances of time travel into the future are slim. What about travel into the past? This, as we shall presently see, is a somewhat different story, causing even weirder clashes with our "normal," common-sense view of reality.

Suppose a team of detectives arrives at the scene of a crime and starts investigating. This means following the cause-effect chains backward in time, i.e., from the here and now into the past. It does not seem entirely absurd to call this activity a travel back in time, at least not as long as we mean a gathering of information in that part of our space-time continuum that has already disappeared. If the investigators are successful, they will detect the causal connections leading them back to the moment of the crime, and there they will "meet" its author, even though this will be only one of his "former selves" and even though his "present self" will at the moment be elsewhere. (The detectives' next job will be to follow the causal chains from the scene of the crime forward in time and catch up with the criminal.)

But this is not quite what time travelers in science fiction do. They somehow reverse the motion picture and let the film projector run backward. Surprisingly, such a time reversal is not entirely ruled out by theoretical physics. The special theory of relativity shows that anything traveling at a speed greater than light must go backward in time.* (In the footnote on page 176 we already considered some of the weird time distortions that would occur if the speed of a spaceship were to *approach* that of light.) Physicists have postulated the existence of faster-than-light particles, called tachyons, and large sums of money have already been spent in various attempts to detect them. If tachyons were found, and if they could be used as signals, very unsettling paradoxes of communication would arise. Consider the following diagram.

---

* Martin Gardner has written a delightful article on this subject [51].

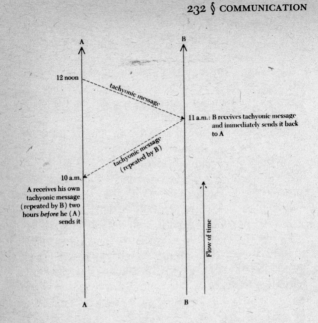

This represents the exchange of a tachyonic message between A and B, who are separated by a fairly large distance in space. Since they both (together with the rest of the universe) move in time, their movement is represented by two vertical lines moving upward (a line being an infinite number of points). At 12 noon a tachyonic message is beamed from A to B informing B of an event that has just taken place. Since the message travels backward in time, it reaches B at 11 o'clock; that is, it gets there an hour before it is sent. This also means that when B gets the signal, it informs him of an event that has not yet taken place. He therefore has true precognition. Without wasting any time, B now repeats the message back to A, whom it reaches at 10 o'clock. With the receipt of this message, A is now in possession of information relating to an event that will take place in two hours—a mind-boggling state of affairs, especially if we bear in mind that he himself is the originator of the message.

The paradoxes resulting from the use of faster-than-light particles for communication were first described by the physicist Richard C. Tolman in 1917 [171]. His ideas were the basis of a paper written by G. A. Benford, D. L. Book and W. A. Newcomb (the author of the Newcomb Paradox), researchers at the Lawrence Radiation Laboratory in California [19]. They suggested that the search for tachyons has so far produced no results because—to paraphrase their argument in lay language—the faster-than-light nature of the tachyons means that the normal *if-then* nature of the experiment is reversed and becomes a *then-if*, so to speak. In other words, the observation (nature's answer) would always arrive before the experiment (the question put to nature), just as on a tachyonic antitelephone (as Benford and his colleagues have appropriately called such a futuristic device), the answers would always arrive before the questions were spoken. Therefore, if such communication takes place, it cannot take place,° and by the same token, if successful tachyonic experiments can be conducted, they have to be unsuccessful—which, indeed, they have been so far.

The ultimate in science-fiction time travel is, of course, the use of an actual time machine, as described in Wells's classic story. And while its construction may be a thing of the distant future, the logical problems raised by the use of such an imaginary machine are with us today, and like Maxwell's Demon, lead us into a deeper understanding of the relativity of our world view.

Consider the left side of the filmstrip-like diagram at the top of page 235. It shows our time traveler's life from his

° Notice the similarity between this communicational impasse and Popper's prediction paradox (page 16).

appearance in time (his birth) up to an age of about thirty. At this time he has completed his intricate time machine and takes a trip back into the past (shown by the slanted line running down and to the right). This is meant to show that he has not simply put the film projector in reverse and is watching the motion picture of his life run backward, but that he is actually traveling against the flow of time. He goes back about fifteen years (which takes him only a few minutes, let us assume), stops the machine and gets off, thus re-entering the time flow (the filmstrip at the right) at a point when he himself is (was) fifteen years old. If he merely looks around without producing any effects—that is, without inserting himself in any way into causality by doing something or communicating with somebody—nothing strange will happen. But the moment he starts to interact, amusing and mind-bending consequences follow. Suppose, Reichenbach [142, 143] suggests, he meets his former self, and they start a conversation. He knows that the young man is his former self, but to the young man he is simply an older man who possesses a disturbing amount of information about his (the younger man's) life and even (nonchalantly or with annoying insistence, I imagine) makes predictions about the future. He even predicts that the young man will one day meet his former self. In all likelihood, the younger will dismiss all this as coming from an insane person and leave him. This, as we have seen earlier, is about the best thing he can do; if he takes the older man seriously, there is no way of telling what the consequences will be.

Imagine that you know the young man and have had occasion to follow his life since birth. This fact can be represented by placing a (preferably transparent) ruler on the diagram, parallel to the space line on the bottom, and moving it slowly upward. This is your own motion within, and together with, the stream of time. At a certain moment (i.e., when the edge of the ruler arrives at the beginning of

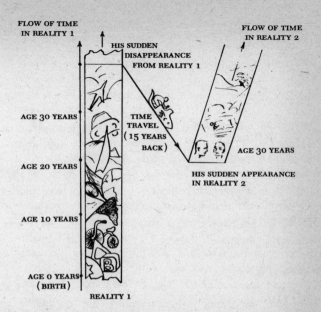

FLOW OF TIME
IN REALITY 1

FLOW OF TIME
IN REALITY 2

HIS SUDDEN
DISAPPEARANCE
FROM REALITY 1

AGE 30 YEARS

TIME
TRAVEL
(15 YEARS
BACK)

AGE 30 YEARS

AGE 20 YEARS

HIS SUDDEN APPEARANCE
IN REALITY 2

AGE 10 YEARS

AGE 0 YEARS
(BIRTH)

REALITY 1

the left-hand time track) the child is born. You and he now travel together in the stream of time until, at about his fifteenth birthday, something very strange happens: a thirty-year-old version of him suddenly appears out of the thin air and joins the two of you and the rest of the universe. This is, of course, the moment at which your ruler touches the right-hand time track. As you continue to move it upward, two lives unfold before your very eyes, or if you prefer, two realities coexist and develop at the same time, but develop quite differently, as implied by the slanting upward direction of the right-hand time track. What you can see in the diagram but not in actual fact is the time traveler on his machine. He is going backward in time and is therefore invisible. By the time your friend's younger self reaches the age of thirty, he disappears as inexplicably as his older self appeared out of nowhere fifteen years ago.°

° The diagrammatic representation used in this illustration is called a Feynman graph, after its author, Nobel Prize-winner Richard Feynman

All of this seems quite unbelievable, but it is neither illogical nor conceptually impossible. Once we start tampering with time, even if only as an intellectual exercise, we find that our language, and with it our thinking processes, begin to let us down very quickly. Small wonder, for any language is, of course, based on the language user's definition of reality and, in turn, determines and perpetuates this definition. In one of his articles [55], Martin Gardner has assembled an impressive anthology of examples from science fiction, all dealing in one way or another with the strange contradictions of time travel, especially when interaction (communication) is allowed to take place and objects are carried from the present to the past or the future. Let me quote just one of these examples:

In Fredric Brown's short story "Experiment," Professor Johnson has developed a small-scale experimental model of a time machine. Small articles placed on it can be sent into the past or the future. He first demonstrates to his two colleagues a five-minute time travel into the future, by setting the future-dial and placing a small brass cube on the machine's platform. It instantly vanishes and reappears five minutes later. The next experiment, five minutes into the past, is a little trickier. Professor Johnson explains that having set the past-dial at five minutes, he will place the cube on the platform at exactly 3 o'clock. But since time is now running backward, it should vanish from his hand and appear on the platform at five minutes before 3; that is, five minutes before he places it there. One of his colleagues asks the obvious question: "How can you place it there, then?" The professor explains that at 3 o'clock the cube will vanish

---

[42]. In such a graph, space (in all its three dimensions) is represented in simplified form on the horizontal line (the X axis of the graph), and time at a right angle to it, running upward on the Y axis. See also Gerald Feinberg's paper on particles that go faster than light [41].

from the platform and appear in his hand, to be placed on the machine. This is exactly what happens. The second colleague wants to know what would happen if, after the cube has appeared on the platform (five minutes before being placed there), Johnson were to change his mind and not put it there at 3 o'clock. Would this not create a paradox?

"An interesting idea," Professor Johnson said.
"I had not thought of it and it will be interesting to try. Very well, I shall *not* . . ."
There was no paradox at all. The cube remained.
But the entire rest of the Universe, professors and all, vanished. [22]

Another possibility is the one already mentioned in connection with the filmstrip illustration: every time a time traveler enters the past, the universe splits into two time tracks. One of them is the continuation of the way things have been going; the other is the start of a totally new reality in which history may take a totally different course.° The cartoon on the following page is an illustration of this possibility, involving both space and time travel.

Gardner's article begins and ends with a reference to James Joyce's novel *Finnegans Wake*, in which the river Liffey, flowing through Dublin, is the great symbol of time:

Physicists are taking more interest than ever before in what philosophers have said about time, thinking harder

---

° And this is precisely what would have to happen when Newcomb's Being comes back from the future (where he observed your choice regarding the two boxes) and places (or does not place) the $1 million in Box 2. The very fact of bringing back "correct" information from the future into the present creates a new reality in which the foreknowledge may no longer be correct.

"Miss! Oh, Miss! For God's sake, stop!"

than ever before about what it means to say time has a "direction" and what connection, if any, this all has with human consciousness and will. Is history like a vast "river-run" that can be seen by God or the gods from source to mouth, or from an infinite past to an infinite future, in one timeless and eternal glance? Is freedom of will no more than an illusion as the current of existence propels us into a future that in some unknown sense already exists? To vary the metaphor, is history a pre-recorded motion picture, projected on the four-dimensional screen of our space-time for the amusement or edification of some unimaginable Audience?

Or is the future, as William James and others have so passionately argued, open and undetermined, not existing in *any* sense until it actually happens? Does the future bring genuine novelty—surprises that even the gods are unable to anticipate? Such questions go far beyond the reach of physics and probe aspects of existence that we are as little capable of comprehending as the fish in the river Liffey are of comprehending the city of Dublin. [51]

20

The Perennial Now

Quia tempus non erit amplius
(That time shall be no longer).

Apocalypse 10:6

If oil is poured from one vessel into another, it flows in an arc of utter smoothness and silence. To the beholder there is something fascinating in the glasslike, motionless appearance of this rapid flow. Perhaps it reminds us of that aspect of time whose mysteries are even greater than those of the future and of the past—the infinitely short present, wedged in between these two infinitely long expanses extending in opposite directions. It is both our most immediate and our most intangible experience of reality. Now has no length, yet it is the only point in time at which what happens, happens and what changes, changes. It is past before we can even become aware of it and yet, since every present moment is immediately followed by a new present moment, Now is our only direct experience of reality—hence the Zen Buddhistic simile of the oil stream.

Like the Square in Flatland who could not grasp the nature of a three-dimensional solid except in terms of a movement in time, we cannot conceive of time as a fourth dimension except through the image of a flow. Our mind cannot grasp time in the Parmenidean sense of "whole, unique, immovable, all at once . . ." except under very special circumstances and for very fleeting moments. Rightly or wrongly, these are called mystical. There are countless descriptions of them, and different as the descriptions may be, their authors seem to agree that they are somehow timeless and more real than reality.

Dostoevski's Prince Myshkin (*The Idiot*) is an epileptic. As with many of his fellow sufferers, the last few seconds (the so-called aura) preceding a grand mal seizure reveal to him this reality:

> At that moment I seem somehow to understand that extraordinary saying that *there shall be no more time*. Probably this is the very second that was not long enough for the water to be spilt out of Mahomet's pitcher, though the epileptic prophet had time to gaze at all the habitations of Allah.*

But the perennial Now is hardly ever perceived without the distortions and contaminations introduced into it by the mind from past experience and future expectations. Throughout this book we have seen how assumptions, beliefs, premises, superstitions, hopes and the like may become more real than reality, creating that web of delusions called *maya* in Indian philosophy. Thus, to empty himself, to free himself from the involvement with past and future, is the goal of the mystic. "The Sufi," writes the

* It is reported that when Allah's messenger entered the prophet's tent to show him the seven heavens, Mahomet upon rising overturned a pitcher standing by the side of his resting place.

thirteenth-century Persian poet Jalal-ud-din Rumi, "is the son *of time present.*" And Omar Khayyám longs for deliverance from past and future, albeit by means of yet another delusion, when he sings: "Ah, my beloved, fill the cup that *clears today of past regrets and future fears.*"

The experience of the perennial Now is not entirely limited to auras or intoxication, however. Moments of great peace or fulfillment as well as, paradoxically, states of great danger are conducive to its occurrence. It happened to Koestler in the death cell of a Spanish prison while he was occupying his mind with the intellectual elegance of Euclid's proof that the number of primes is infinite:

> [It] swept over me like a wave. The wave had originated in an articulate verbal insight; but this evaporated at once, leaving in its wake only a wordless essence, a fragrance of eternity, a quiver of the arrow in the blue. I must have stood there for some minutes, entranced, with a wordless awareness that "this is perfect—perfect." . . . Then I was floating on my back in a river of peace, under bridges of silence. It came from nowhere and flowed nowhere. Then there was no river and no I. The I had ceased to exist. . . . When I say "the I had ceased to exist," I refer to a concrete experience that is verbally as incommunicable as the feeling aroused by a piano concerto, yet just as real—only much more real. In fact, its primary mark is the sensation that this state is more real than any other one has experienced before. [79]

And here is a final paradox. All those who have tried to express the experience of the pure Now have found language to be woefully inadequate. "The Tao that can be expressed is not the real Tao," wrote Lao Tzu 2,500 years ago. When master Shin-t'ou was asked to explain the ultimate teaching of Buddhism, he answered, "You won't understand it until you have it." Of course, once you have it, you won't need an explanation. And Wittgenstein, having pushed his inquiry into reality to the limits of the human mind, concluded his *Tractatus* with the famous sentence "Whereof one cannot speak, thereof one must be silent."

This, then, is a good place to conclude this book.

Bibliographical Notes

1. Edwin A. Abbott, *Flatland: A Romance in Many Dimensions.* 6th ed. (New York, Dover, 1952).
2. *Op. cit.*, p. 64.
3. *Op. cit.*, p. 66.
4. *Op. cit.*, p. 80.
5. Joe K. Adams, "Laboratory Studies of Behavior Without Awareness." *Psychological Bulletin*, 4:383–408 (1957).
6. Anthony Alpers, *Dolphins* (London, John Murray, 1960).
7. *Op. cit.*, p. 212.
8. Robert Ardrey, *The Social Contract: A Personal Enquiry into the Evolutionary Sources of Order and Disorder* (New York, Atheneum, 1970), p. 130.
9. Solomon E. Asch, "Opinions and Social Pressure." *Scientific American*, 193:31–35 (November 1955).
10. ———, *Social Psychology* (New York, Prentice-Hall, 1952), pp. 450–83 *(passim)*.

11. Solomon E. Asch, "Studies of Independence and Submission to Group Pressures." *Psychological Monographs*, Vol. 70, No. 416 (1956).

12. Isaac Asimov, *The End of Eternity* (Greenwich, Conn., Fawcett, 1955), pp. 186–87.

13. Gregory Bateson, Don D. Jackson, Jay Haley and John H. Weakland, "Toward a Theory of Schizophrenia." *Behavioral Science*, 1:251–64 (1956).

14. Gregory Bateson and Don D. Jackson, "Some Varieties of Pathogenic Organization." In David McK. Rioch and E. A. Weinstein, eds., *Disorders of Communication*, Vol. 42, Research Publications. Association for Research in Nervous and Mental Diseases (Baltimore, Williams & Wilkins, 1964), pp. 270–83.

15. Gregory Bateson, *Steps to an Ecology of Mind* (New York, Ballantine, 1972), p. 367.

16. *Op. cit.*, p. 159.

17. Gregory Bateson, personal communication.

18. Alex Bavelas, personal communication.

19. G. A. Benford, D. L. Book and William A. Newcomb, "The Tachyonic Antitelephone." *Physical Review D*, third series, 2:263–65 (1970).

20. Ladislav Bittman, *The Deception Game* (Syracuse, Syracuse University Research Corporation, 1972).

21. Ronald N. Bracewell, "Communications from Superior Galactic Communities." *Nature*, 186:670–71 (1960).

22. Fredric Brown, "The Experiment." In *Honeymoon in Hell* (New York, Bantam, 1958), pp. 67–68.

23. G. Spencer Brown, *Probability and Scientific Inference* (New York, Longmans, Green, 1957), p. 105.

24. *Op. cit.*, pp. 111–12.

25. *Op. cit.*, pp. 113–15.

26. G. Spencer Brown, *Laws of Form* (New York, Bantam, 1972).

27. *Op. cit.*, p. xiii.

28. C. Maxwell Cade, *Other Worlds Than Ours* (New York, Taplinger, 1967), p. 166.

29. *Op. cit.*, p. 175.

30. Herb Caen, *San Francisco Chronicle* (February 2, 1973), p. 25.

31. Colin Cherry, *On Human Communication* (New York, Science Editions, 1961), p. 120.

32. Ed. Claperède, "Die gelehrten Pferde von Elberfeld." *Tierseele, Blätter für vgl. Seelenkunde* (1914), as quoted by Hediger [64].

33. Giuseppe Cocconi and Philip Morrison, "Searching for Interstellar Communications." *Nature*, 184:844–46 (1959).

34. Norman Cohn, *Warrant for Genocide* (London, Eyre & Spottiswoode, 1967), pp. 74–75.

35. Charles Cros, *Étude sur les moyens de communication avec les planètes*. As quoted in Louis Forestier, *Charles Cros, l'homme et l'oeuvre* (Paris, Lettres Modernes, 1963), p. 64.

36. Feodor M. Dostoevski, *The Brothers Karamazov*, trans. by Constance Garnett (New York, The Modern Library, n.d.).

37. *Op. cit.*, pp. 303–24 *(passim)*.

38. Robert B. Ekvall, *Faithful Echo* (New York, Twayne, 1960), pp. 109–13 *(passim)*.

39. Milton H. Erickson, "The Confusion Technique in Hypnosis." *American Journal of Clinical Hypnosis*, 6:183–207 (1964). Reprinted in Jay Haley, ed., *Advanced Techniques of Hypnosis and Therapy: Selected Papers of Milton H. Erickson* (New York, Grune & Stratton, 1967), pp. 130–57.

40. Aaron Esterson, *The Leaves of Spring* (Harmondsworth, Penguin, 1972).

41. Gerald Feinberg, "Particles That Go Faster Than Light." *Scientific American*, 222:69–77 (February 1970).

42. Richard P. Feynman, "The Theory of Positrons." *Physical Review*, 76:749–59 (1949).

43. Roger Fouts and Randall L. Rigby, "Man-Chimpanzee Communication." In T. A. Seboek, ed., *How Animals Communicate* (Bloomington, Indiana University Press, 1975).

44. Roger Fouts, personal communication.

45. Hans Freudenthal, *Lincos: Design of a Language for Cosmic Intercourse*, Part I (Amsterdam, North-Holland Publishing Co., 1960).

46. Karl von Frisch, "Dialects in the Language of the Bees." *Scientific American* 207:79–87 (August 1962).

47. Beatrice T. Gardner and R. Allen Gardner, "Two-way Communication with an Infant Chimpanzee." In Allan M. Schrier and Fred Stollnitz, eds., *Behavior of Non-human Primates* (New York, Academic Press, 1971).

48. *Op. cit.*, p. 167.

49. *Op. cit.*, p. 172.

50. *Op. cit.*, p. 176.

51. Martin Gardner, "Can Time Go Backward?" *Scientific American*, 216:98–108 (January 1967).

52. ———, "On the Meaning of Randomness and Some Ways to Achieve It." *Scientific American* 219:116–21 (July 1968).

53. ———, "Free Will Revisited, With a Mind-bending Prediction Paradox by William Newcomb." *Scientific American*, 229:104–9 (July 1973).

54. ———, "Reflections on Newcomb's Problem: A Prediction and Free-will Dilemma." *Scientific American*, 230:102–8 (March 1974).

55. ———, "On the Contradictions of Time Travel." *Scientific American*, 230:120–23 (May 1974).

56. R. Allen Gardner and Beatrice T. Gardner, "Teaching Sign Language to a Chimpanzee." *Science*, 165:664–72 (1969).

57. Thomas H. Gillespie, *The Story of the Edinburgh Zoo* (Old Castle, M. Slains, 1964).

58. Kurt Gödel, "Über formal unentscheidbare Sätze der Principia Mathematica und verwandter Systeme, I." *Monatshefte für Mathematik und Physik*, 38:173–98 (1931). English translation: *On Formally Undecidable Propositions of Principia Mathematica and Related Systems, I* (Edinburgh and London, Oliver and Boyd, 1962).

59. Cathy Hayes, *The Ape in Our House* (New York, Harper, 1951).

60. *Op. cit.*, p. 83.

61. *Op. cit.*, p. 101.

62. Keith Hayes and Catherine Hayes, "The Intellectual Development of a Home-raised Chimpanzee." *Proceedings of the American Philosophical Society*, 95:105–9 (1951).

63. Keith Hayes and Catherine Hayes, "Imitation in a Home-raised Chimpanzee." *Journal of Comparative and Physiological Psychology*, 45:450–59 (1952).

64. H. Hediger, "Verstehen und Verständigungsmöglichkeiten zwischen Mensch und Tier." *Schweizerische Zeitschrift für Psychologie und ihre Anwendungen*, 26:234–55 (1967), pp. 239–40.

65. *Op. cit.*, p. 240.

66. Joseph Heller, *Catch-22* (New York, Dell, 1955), pp. 46–47.

67. Eugen Herrigel, *Zen in the Art of Archery*, trans. by R. F. C. Hill (New York, Pantheon, 1953).

68. Eckhard H. Hess, "Attitude and Pupil Size." *Scientific American*, 212:46–54 (April 1965), p. 46.

69. *Op. cit.*, p. 50.

70. Hermann Hesse, *In Sight of Chaos*, trans. by Stephen Hudson (Zurich, Verlag Seldwyla, 1923), p. 60.

71. Sebastian von Hoerner, "The General Limits of Space Travel." *Science*, 137:18–23 (1962).

72. Lancelot Hogben, "Astroglossa or First Steps in Celestial Syntax." *British Interplanetary Society Journal*, 11:258–74 (November 1952), p. 259.

73. Thomas Hora, "Tao, Zen and Existential Psychotherapy." *Psychologia*, 2:236–42 (1959), p. 237.

74. Nigel Howard, "The Mathematics of Meta-games." *General Systems*, 11:167–86 and 187–200 (1966).

75. Don D. Jackson, "Play, Paradox and People: Identified Flying Objects." *Medical Opinion and Review* (February 1967), pp. 116–25.

76. Franz Kafka, *The Trial* (New York, Knopf, 1953), pp. 268–79.

77. David Kahn, *The Codebreakers* (New York, Macmillan, 1967).

78. S. A. Kaplan, ed., *Extraterrestrial Civilizations: Problems of Interstellar Communication*. Translated from Russian (Jerusalem, Israel Program for Scientific Translations, 1971). (Available from U.S. Department of Commerce, National Technical Information Service, Springfield, Va. 22151. NASA Publication TT F-631.)

79. Arthur Koestler, *The Invisible Writing* (New York, Macmillan, 1969), p. 429.

80. Ronald D. Laing, *The Self and Others* (London, Tavistock, 1961).

81. Ronald D. Laing, H. Phillipson and A. Russell Lee, *Interpersonal Perception* (New York, Springer, 1966), pp. 17–18.

82. Ronald D. Laing, "Mystification, Confusion and Conflict." In Ivan Boszormenyi-Nagy and James L. Framo, eds., *Intensive Family Therapy: Theoretical and Practical Aspects* (New York, Harper, 1965), pp. 343–63.

83. ———, *Knots* (New York, Pantheon, 1970), p. 55.

84. ——— and Aaron Esterson, *Sanity, Madness and the Family*, Vol. I, *Families of Schizophrenics* (London, Tavistock, 1964).

85. Pierre Simon de Laplace, *A Philosophical Essay on Probabilities*, trans. from the 6th edition by Frederick Wilson Truscott and Frederick Lincoln Emory (New York, Dover, 1951), p. 4.

86. Lawick-Goodall, Jane van, *In the Shadow of Man* (Boston, Houghton Mifflin, 1971).

87. Leslie, Robert Franklin, "The Bear That Came for Supper." *Reader's Digest*, 85:75–79 (1964).

88. John C. Lilly, *Man and Dolphin* (Garden City, N.Y., Doubleday, 1961), pp. 55 and 203.

89. ———, *The Mind of the Dolphin* (Garden City, N.Y., Doubleday, 1967), p. 115.

90. *Op. cit.*, p. 301.

91. John C. Lilly, "The Dolphin Experience." Taped lecture (cassette). Big Sur Recordings, n.d.

92. Duncan A. Lunan, "Space Probe from Epsilon Boötis." *Spaceflight*, 15:122–31 (April 1973).

93. *Op. cit.*, p. 123.

94. John W. Macvey, *Whispers from Space* (New York, Macmillan, 1973), p. 152.

95. *Op. cit.*, p. 226.

96. J. C. Masterman, *The Double-Cross System in the War of 1939 to 1945* (New Haven, Yale University Press, 1972).

97. *Op. cit.*, p. 2.

98. *Op. cit.*, p. 9.

99. *Op. cit.*, pp. 30–31.

100. *Op. cit.*, p. 88.

101. Sergey Mikhalkov, *Der Spiegel*, 28:87 (February 4, 1974).

102. Jacques Monod, *Chance and Necessity*, trans. by Austrin Wainhouse (New York, Vintage, 1972).

103. *Op. cit.*, pp. 118–19.

104. Ewen E. S. Montagu, *The Man Who Never Was* (New York, Bantam, 1969).

105. *Op. cit.*, p. 27.

106. *Op. cit.*, p. 40.

107. *Op. cit.*, p. 107.

108. *Op. cit.*, pp. 133–34.

109. Edgar Morin, *Rumour in Orléans*, trans. by Peter Green (New York, Pantheon, 1971).

110. *Op. cit.*, pp. 17–18.

111. *Op. cit.*, pp. 30–31.

113. *Op. cit.*, p. 165.

114. *Op. cit.*, pp. 255–56.

115. W. H. Morse and B. F. Skinner, "A Second Type of Superstition in the Pigeon." *American Journal of Psychology*, 70:308–11 (1957).

116. Ernst Nagel and James R. Newman, *Gödel's Proof* (New York, New York University Press, 1958).

117. James R. Newman, *The World of Mathematics* (New York, Simon & Schuster, 1956), p. 2383.

118. Robert Nozick, "Newcomb's Problem and the Two Principles of Choice." In Nicholas Rescher, ed., *Essays in Honor of Carl G. Hempel* (Dordrecht, Holland, D. Reidel Publishing, 1970), pp. 114–46. (Distributed in U.S.A. and Canada by Humanities Press, New York.) (See also [54].)

119. Bernard M. Oliver, "Radio Search for Distant Races." *International Science and Technology*, No. 10 (October 1962), pp. 55–61.

120. Bernard M. Oliver, personal communication.

121. Parmenides, *The Way of Truth*. Fragment 8, 4–6.

122. Penny Patterson, personal communication.

123. Y. I. Perelman, *Myeshplanyetnye puteshestvuiya* [Interplan-

etary Voyages]. 6th ed. (Moscow and Leningrad, Government Press, 1929).

124. Oskar Pfungst, *Das Pferd des Herrn von Osten (Der Kluge Hans)* (Leipzig, Johann Ambrosius Bart, 1907. For English edition, see [125]).

125. ———, *Clever Hans: The Horse of Mr. von Osten*, Robert Rosenthal, ed. (New York, Rinehart & Winston, 1965).

126. *Op. cit.*, p. 13.

127. *Op. cit.*, p. 261.

128. *Op. cit.*, pp. 262–63.

129. Max Planck, *A Scientific Autobiography and Other Papers*, trans. by Frank Gaynor (London, Williams & Norgate, 1950), p. 75.

130. Pliny the Younger, *Epistulae*. Librum IX, epist. 33. (My translation.)

131. Dusko Popov, *Spy/Counterspy*, with a foreword by Ewen Montagu (New York, Grosset & Dunlap, 1974), pp. 162–219.

132. *Op. cit.*, p. 267.

133. Sir Karl Raimund Popper, *Conjectures and Refutations: The Growth of Scientific Knowledge* (New York, Basic Books, 1962).

134. ———, "A Comment on the New Prediction Paradox." *British Journal for the Philosophy of Science*, 13:51 (1963).

135. ———, *The Open Society and Its Enemies* (New York, Harper Torchbooks, 1963), p. 200.

136. David Premack, "Language in Chimpanzee?" *Science*, 172:808–22 (1971).

137. *Project Cyclops: A Design Study of a System for Detecting Extraterrestrial Life*. Publication No. CR 114445; rev. ed. 7/73 (NASA/Ames Research Center, Code LT, Moffett Field, Calif. 94035), p. 4.

138. *Op. cit.*, pp. 179–80.

139. Anatol Rapoport and Albert M. Chammah, with the collaboration of Carol J. Orwant, *Prisoner's Dilemma: A Study in Conflict and Cooperation* (Ann Arbor, University of Michigan Press, 1965).

140. Anatol Rapoport, "Escape from Paradox." *Scientific American*, 217:50–56 (July 1967).

141. Hans Reichenbach, *The Direction of Time*, ed. by Maria Reichenbach (Berkeley, University of California Press, 1956), p. 11.

142. *Op. cit.*, p. 37.

143. Hans Reichenbach, *The Philosophy of Space and Time* (New York, Dover, 1957), pp. 140–42.

144. R. B. Robinson, *On Whales and Men* (New York, Knopf, 1954), as quoted by Lilly [88], pp. 93–94.

145. Robert Rosenthal, *Experimenter Effects in Behavioral Research* (New York, Appleton-Century-Crofts, 1966).

146. Jürgen Ruesch and Gregory Bateson, *Communication: The Social Matrix of Psychiatry* (New York, Norton, 1951), pp. 212–27.

147. D. Rumbaugh, T. V. Gill and E. C. von Glaserfeld, "Reading and Sentence Completion by a Chimpanzee (Pan)." *Science*, 182:731–33 (1973).

148. Nikolai A. Rynin, *Myeshplanyetnye soobshchenia*, III: *Luchistaya energiya v fantasiyakh romanistov i v proyetakh uchenykh* [Interplanetary Communication, Vol. III: Radiant Energy in the Fantasies of the Novelists and in the Projects of Scientists]. (Leningrad, Izdatel'stvo P.P. Soikin, 1930).

149. Carl Sagan, *The Cosmic Connection*. Produced by Jerome Agel (Garden City, N.Y., Anchor Press, Doubleday, 1973), pp. 19–20.

150. *Op. cit.*, p. 25.

151. Carl Sagan, ed., *Communication with Extraterrestrial Intelligence (CETI)* (Cambridge, MIT Press, 1973), pp. 183 and 318.

152. L. Salzman, "Reply to Critics." *International Journal of Psychiatry*, 6:473–76 (1968).

153. Walter Schellenberg, *The Labyrinth*, trans. by Louis Hagen (New York, Harper, 1956).

154. Thomas C. Schelling, *The Strategy of Conflict* (Cambridge, Harvard University Press, 1960).

155. *Op. cit.*, p. 54.

156. *Op. cit.*, p. 56.

157. *Op. cit.*, p. 148.

158. Thomas C. Schelling, "Reciprocal Measures for Arms Stabilization." Reprinted in Richard A. Faulk and Saul H. Mendlovitz, eds., *The Strategy of World Order*, Vol. IV, *Disarmament and Economic Development* (New York, World Law Fund, 1966), pp. 127–28.

159. Peter Schmid, "Der japanische Hamlet." *Der Monat*, 18:5–10 (August 1966), p. 7.

160. Arthur Schopenhauer, *Über den Willen in der Natur*. In *Arthur Schopenhauers sämtliche Werke*, Vol. III (Munich, R. Piper, 1912), p. 346. (My translation.)

161. Joseph Schreieder, *Das war das Englandspiel* (Munich, Walter Stutz, 1950).

162. *Op. cit.*, p. 402.

163. *Op. cit.*, p. 403.

164. I. S. Shklovsky, "The Lifetimes of Technical Civilizations." In Carl Sagan, ed., *Communication with Extraterrestrial Intelligence (CETI)* (Cambridge, MIT Press, 1973), p. 148.

165. B. F. Skinner, " 'Superstition' in the Pigeon." *Journal of Experimental Psychology*, 38:168–72 (1948).

166. Carlos E. Sluzki, Janet Beavin, Alejandro Tarnopolsky and Eliseo Verón, "Transactional Disqualification." *Archives of General Psychiatry*, 16:494–504 (1967).

167. Carlos E. Sluzki and Eliseo Verón, "The Double Bind as a Universal Pathogenic Situation." *Family Process*, 10:397–410 (1971).

168. Carlos E. Sluzki and Donald C. Ransom, eds., *Double Bind: The Foundation of the Communicational Approach to the Family* (New York, Grune & Stratton, 1975).

169. R. Sommer, *Tierpsychologie* (Leipzig, Quelle & Meyer, 1925).

170. Carl Størmer, "Short Wave Echos and the Aurora Borealis." *Nature*, No. 3079, 122:681 (1928).

171. Richard C. Tolman, *The Theory of Relativity of Motion* (Berkeley, University of California Press, 1917), pp. 54–55.

172. Pamela L. Travers, *Mary Poppins* (New York, Harcourt, Brace, 1934).

173. Daniele Varé, *Laughing Diplomat* (New York, Doubleday, Doran, 1938), p. 381.

174. Paul Watzlawick, Janet H. Beavin and Don D. Jackson, *Pragmatics of Human Communication* (New York, Norton, 1967).

175. *Op. cit.*, pp. 39–43 and 94–96.

176. *Op. cit.*, pp. 54–59 and 93–99.

177. *Op. cit.*, pp. 96–99.

178. *Op. cit.*, pp. 131–32.

179. *Op. cit.*, pp. 219–29.

180. Paul Watzlawick, "Patterns of Psychotic Communication." In Pierre Doucet and Camille Laurin, eds., *Problems of Psychosis*, Part I (Amsterdam, Excerpta Medica Foundation, 1969), pp. 51–52.

181. Paul Watzlawick, John H. Weakland and Richard Fisch. *Change: Principles of Problem Formation and Problem Resolution* (New York, Norton, 1974).

182. *Op. cit.*, pp. 34–35.

183. *Op. cit.*, pp. 35–36.

184. *Op. cit.*, pp. 47–61.

185. *Op. cit.*, pp. 62–73.

186. *Op. cit.*, pp. 92–109.

187. Ludwig Wittgenstein, *Tractatus Logico-Philosophicus* (New York, Humanities Press, 1951), p. 151.

188. Forrest G. Wood, "Porpoise Play." *Mariner* [mimeographed house organ of Marine Studios], (March 1954), p. 4., as quoted in [6], p. 100.

189. John C. Wright, *Problem Solving and Search Behavior under Noncontingent Rewards.* Unpublished dissertation, Stanford University, 1960.

190. ———, "Consistency and Complexity of Response Sequences as a Function of Schedules of Noncontingent Reward." *Journal of Experimental Psychology*, 63:601–9 (1962).

191. Robert M. Yerkes and Blanche W. Learned, *Chimpanzee Intelligence and Its Vocal Expression* (Baltimore, Williams & Wilkins, 1925), p. 53.

(Page numbers in bold print refer to definitions.)

About the Author

PAUL WATZLAWICK, research associate at the Mental Research Institute in Palo Alto and clinical associate professor in the Department of Psychiatry, Stanford University, was born in Austria, received his Ph.D. in philosophy and modern languages from Cà Foscari University, Venice, Italy, and studied psychotherapy at the C. G. Jung Institute in Zurich. He has been professor of psychotherapy at the University of El Salvador, Central America, a research associate at Temple University Medical Center in Philadelphia and guest lecturer at many universities and training institutes in the United States, Canada, Europe and Latin America. He is principal author of *Pragmatics of Human Communication* and *Change*.

VINTAGE WORKS OF SCIENCE AND PSYCHOLOGY

VINTAGE HISTORY—WORLD